SHIP
SHAPE

What Sailing Can Tell Us About the Art of Business Leadership and Strategy

Nick Bashford
Business leader, yachtsman and author

First Published and distributed in the United Kingdom by:
Nyetimber Publishing
The Cabin, 9 Lion Road, Nyetimber, West Sussex, PO21 3JZ
nick@nyetimbermanagement.co.uk

©Nick Bashford 2021

The author asserts the moral right to be identified
as the author of this work.

All rights reserved. No part of this publication may be reproduced, stored in a retrieval system, or transmitted in any form or by any means, electronic, mechanical, photocopying, recording or otherwise, without the prior permission of the publisher.

A catalogue record for the book is available from the British Library.

ISBN 978-1-5272-9865-1

Printed in the United Kingdom by
Biddles Books, Kings Lynn, Norfolk, PE32 1SF

What others say about SHIPSHAPE

This is a book which should, at all times, be within easy reach of anyone with leadership pretensions. It's right on target.

Robert Glossop MBE

The way that Nick integrates the story of the Fastnet race (and anecdotes from his sailing experiences) provides light relief but also subtly teaches the reader about leadership and teamwork while avoiding a more staid and linear approach to business coaching. As parables impart wisdom through storytelling, this manages to capture the essence of his philosophy without actually 'teaching' in a didactic and obvious way. He has a light touch when it comes to his style of writing – relaxed and friendly - and I was always keen to hear what happened next which kept me present in the moment and engaged in the narrative. Having read a lot of business books, I was happy to report that this one was consistently interesting and fun but it also made me reflect. The questions at the end of each chapter encourage the reader to interact and embed the insights without demanding too much of them. I also like the fact it's concise and snappy. This is just the sort of quick, big picture read that a busy business leader will want to (and have time to) dip into.

Sarah Busby, Development Editor

When reading this book, I had many moments when I realized that, after (40) years as a business owner, I could have used Nick's advice numerous times during my company's initial growth, early successes, rapid uncontrolled growth, near failure and, finally, its total rebirth. Nick realizes the perfect balance of having competent managers who work as a team, focused on the same goal, and who stay in their lane under the direction of an owner who has set clear objectives and gives their managers the proper tools as well as the authority to do their job in a positive and supportive environment.

In sum, I believe this book should not be read once and then put away. It should sit on your credenza as your go-to reminder to refocus your goals and objectives during both stormy and calm waters. It is always easy to navigate in calm waters, but it takes a clear mind and knowledge to brave the storms that day-to-day business throws at you. Nick has always been the captain who can be called upon at any time to set the ship straight.

Joe Hickson Jr.
President, JMH Consulting LLC, USA

Contents

Acknowledgements	vii
Foreword by Stephen Bungay	ix
Author Preface	xiii
Introduction	xv
The Story of the Fastnet Race, Part 1: Finding My Team	**1**
Chapter 1: Finding Your Leadership Framework: The High Alignment and High Autonomy Model	7
The Story of the Fastnet Race, Part 2: Coming Together	**17**
Chapter 2: What's Driving Your Business – People or Process?	29
Chapter 3: The Art of Leadership: Building Trust and Cohesion	33
The Story of the Fastnet Race, Part 3: Working as One	**41**
Chapter 4: Recruiting the Right People	47
Chapter 5: Developing Your Team	53
The Story of the Fastnet Race, Part 4: The Race	**61**
Chapter 6: Embracing Failure as a Tool	69
The Story of a Novice Skipper	**75**
Chapter 7: The Skipper as Strategic Planner	85
Chapter 8: The Value of Strategic Planning	89
Chapter 9: An Example of a Typical Planning Framework	97
Final Thoughts	109

Acknowledgements

I thank the crew of *Yacht Yoda* for asking me to lead their Fastnet campaign of 2009. They had the depth of character and honesty to expose their vulnerabilities and push their knowledge to its limits, always willing to learn and adapt as a team. They each brought with them their independent skills in pursuit of reaching a desired common goal.

In my business life and over the last four decades, I have had the pleasure of meeting and working with some highly talented people, many of whom became firm friends. I have learnt so much from many good leaders, and I am in debt to those that took a punt on me in my formative years. I would like to especially acknowledge Gill Bashford, Roger Jeffrey, John Ball, John Heathcock and Ron and Barbara Reekie, who are special people and who unselfishly supported me as I developed my early business career.

My secondary school tutor and sailing instructor was a teacher called Don Garmen. Through his patience and understanding of my initial fears as a teenager of being trapped in an upturned sailing dinghy, he ignited a fire in me for all things nautical. Because of his early interjection and guiding hand, he is singularly responsible for my continued love of sailing, 40 years on.

In terms of my sailing career, recognition must go to the team at the Royal Navy Auxiliary Service, both in London and Portsmouth. I received invaluable training delivered at the highest level. The inspirational team of Royal Yachting Association instructors that took me under their wing included Ian Galletti, John Clarke and

SHIPSHAPE

Trevor Clifton. They continue to be a source of inspiration to me, sharing their knowledge, wisdom and stories.

I am grateful to my reading team who made this book possible, as well as the professional help of my editing team, Sarah Busby and Andrew Dawson, both of whom helped to make this short story a reality in print.

Finally, and in particular, I would like to acknowledge my family. I am blessed with having the most supportive of parents and brothers who, to this day, still enjoy a good discussion about the activities that I am involved with. Thank you to my soulmate and fiancée, Sharon, for her absolute support in everything that I do, and to my three beautiful children for keeping me grounded.

Foreword

It has been my pleasure to have known Nick Bashford for some 20 years.

I first met him as his client when he was an entrepreneur running a building company and noted that he was not afraid of mucking in and literally getting his hands dirty when he needed to, always putting my interests first and always delivering a high-quality service. When he moved on to run part of an established company, I was not surprised to see him grow the top and bottom lines of the business by challenging received wisdom whilst taking his management colleagues and his team with him.

I knew of his passion for sailing, but again, I was not surprised when I learned that he had turned it from a personal hobby into a means of developing people. Nick writes that he has two passions: business and sailing. I disagree. He has two others which I think go even deeper: people and leadership. If you want to win yacht races and build a successful business, people and leadership are what it's really all about.

Nick is a man of many parts. He has run his own business, run part of someone else's business, skippered yacht crews and consulted to a range of SMEs. What has enabled him to do all that is a thirst for challenge, boundless optimism and resilience and a desire to learn. He has learned a lot because he does not just get stuff done; he has a rare ability to reflect on his experience. This book tells part of his story and distils the most valuable lessons he has learned so as to make them available to others. We should be grateful for that.

The literature on leadership is vast and constantly growing but most of it is worthless. The core principles of leadership are simple but hard to apply. Developing models and theories usually just complicates things and makes application more difficult. However, a set of stories about 'how I did it', or 'how Jack Welch/Steve Jobs/Jeff Bezos… (fill in your own favourite business hero here) did it' does not help much either because most of us are not like them (thank goodness!). Moreover, what worked – for a time at least – at General Electric, Apple and Amazon won't necessarily work for you. Ultimately, you need some kind of framework to make the lessons transferable.

I'm delighted that Nick has found it helpful to use the alignment and autonomy framework I developed in my book, *The Art of Action,* and uses techniques like backbriefing. I did not invent anything in that book; I just discovered the core principles applied by successful military organisations which have to operate in a fast changing, ambiguous, uncertain and competitive environment, which is what the business landscape is like today. In the book, I track their genesis back 200 years to the time of Napoleon and Nelson. Similar approaches can in fact be found 2,000 years ago in the time of Julius Caesar. That suggests they are pretty robust. Fundamentally, they are about directing, managing and motivating people. *Shipshape* covers all three in a way that brings the principles alive for us today.

Yacht racing is not a metaphor for business. It is another environment in which the principles of leadership and team building needed in business also apply. Using an example from outside business in this way, rather than the business examples Nick might have chosen, helps to focus attention on the essentials without the distraction of wondering whether they are relevant because the business is a different one. The essentials are human universals. Winds, tides, storms and being on a dark ocean at night highlight what they are more clearly than changes in customer demand, new competitors, missed sales targets and office politics.

In reading this book I have discovered something I did not know – how good a writer Nick is. I hope you enjoy reading it as much as I did.

Stephen Bungay
London
June 2021

Author Preface

I would like to share with you a quick snapshot of my background. Hopefully this goes someway to explaining who I am and why it is time to share my thoughts. For the past 40 years, outside the time I spend with my family, I have pursued two other deep passions. They are the sea and the world of business. I have successfully been able to chart a course between the two and, on occasion, I've been lucky enough to combine them at the same time. Skippering thousands of miles with various crews and running business teams on a day-to-day basis has contributed to what I believe is a solid and proven style of leadership, as well as a unique understanding of team dynamics.

During my school education, I developed a passion for sailing and at home I had a deep interest in the world of business. Both sets of grandparents and my parents were running successful family enterprises and I enjoyed working with them during my school holidays. To me, it was inevitable that I would go into business and, on leaving school, I entered the world of insurance. Seeing my early promise and drive, and if the truth be told my appetite for having a chat, my first boss moved me from an administrative role into sales, and I was soon developing and heading up my own sales teams. Within 10 years I was running a multi-million-pound salesforce for a national company, designing and delivering communication and sales training courses to hundreds of direct sales personnel. In the mid-1990s, an opportunity to invest in a new start-up company presented itself. The timing was perfect in terms of my experience, and we successfully grew the business, year on year, turning my initial few thousand pounds of investment into a seven-figure sum when I sold my shares some 12 years later.

During this time, and alongside pursuing my business ambitions, I stayed very close to my passion for sailing through volunteering with a branch of the Royal Navy Reserves, as well as spending much of my spare time sailing yachts. Over the years I built up tens of thousands of skippered sea miles, including making offshore passages as a commercial skipper. Plus, over a five-year period, I instructed more than 350 students in the art of skippering and seamanship. More recently I have been a senior director and advisor to a number of businesses, bringing my wealth of experience and unique management approach to the benefit of these organisations.

I have now captured much of that approach in this short book, which sets out the key components of how to structure your teams and organisation. The focus is about successfully arriving at those all-important strategic gateways. This is not my attempt at teaching experienced, motivated business owners and managers to suck eggs. This book will encourage you to seek out the simple core components of a winning strategy away from the white noise of daily business. I have purposefully not dwelled on any one particular facet of business life, as I acknowledge this is what we do every day. Instead, I have focused on the key ingredients that allow us to have a disciplined and structured journey. A journey that I have successfully completed time and time again, both in business and at sea.

Introduction

I have long been fascinated by the correlation between a well-run yacht and a well-run business. Both require constant reference to direction and positioning. The skipper's role on a yacht is fundamental to your overall success and likelihood of arriving at a chosen destination; the same can be said of the role of a shrewd and inspiring leader in business. I can appreciate why the environment at sea – that can quickly bring out the best and worst in human nature – creates such a unique and rewarding space to test and perfect the art of communication and teamwork. In a high-stakes situation, where everyone relies on one another so implicitly for their safety and the success of the venture, working together efficiently and productively isn't optional – it's essential.

In this book I have attempted to describe the parallels between the expert skipper, their navigation passage plan and a well-led business strategy. How can we take that winning approach to team dynamics into the world of business? There are many motives for sailing the seas, whether it's competitive racing, leisure or employment. There are those that sail far afield on adventures and the commercial skippers and crews who rely on the sea for their livelihoods. Of course, there are also those in the armed forces who patrol and protect our seas. These endeavours all have one thing in common though: they require considered and reasoned leadership alongside high levels of trust and teamwork. I have been fortunate to have had the pleasure of participating in many of the above and have seen and practised, first-hand, the skills required to be successful in this unique environment.

It is said that, in this modern, fast-paced business world, we need to be constantly agile. However, in my opinion, this desire for agility so often comes at the cost of missing the basic principles of success. You certainly have to be agile on the sea, but never at the cost of foregoing the fundamentals that keep you afloat, year in and year out. Leaders need the space and mindset to be constantly ahead of the plan.

So, what are these fundamentals? This book aims to introduce you to the high-level skills of robust leadership that are essential to a rewarding passage at sea as well as in business. In the first part of the book, we discuss the framework of high alignment and high autonomy and the art of leading and motivating your team. This is the foundation that enables cohesion through shared goals and independent working built on trust. I then delve deeper into the importance of valuing people in your business over process, and how investing time into recruiting and developing the right team is the bedrock of a sustainable business. I also consider how failure is a powerful learning tool that enables us to balance creativity, ambition and discipline. Finally, we explore the importance of strategic planning, the leader's role in shaping and embedding it and a successful example of a planning framework. In between these chapters I include storytelling interludes which recall my experiences in the Fastnet race, one of the foremost international sailing challenges.

By interweaving this simple framework of adaptable techniques for business success with my progress in the race, I hope to make clear to you in the following pages the lessons we can draw from this environment. The story of the race neatly typifies the strategies required to fulfil an ambitious plan. Moreover, it is a story full of hope and promise and one which exemplifies the true spirit of collaboration.

Most business professionals dedicate their whole lives to mastering the art of leadership. The value of taking quality time out to read around the subject is paramount if you want to expand your horizons and develop a better understanding of how others operate. If you are a student or a rookie leader in a new start-up, you may want to completely replicate some of the approaches we discuss. For most it is a case of reaffirming what we know to be a core ingredient of success and ensuring that it's embedded in our practice. For some, taking the time out to read this book is an opportunity to step away from the noise of our day-to-day activity, to appraise and challenge the direction we are heading in.

I hope you enjoy the following pages and can take something away of value from the perspectives and insights I have gained.

The Story of the Fastnet Race, Part 1: *Finding My Team*

In 2007, the UK business sector in which I was operating was buoyant so it was a good time to sell the company that I had co-founded some 12 years before. After six months of negotiation, we completed the sale in early 2008, just a few weeks before the worldwide markets crashed (an interesting story for another day). I had been asked, as part of the deal, to remain attached to one of the companies for a period of two years to allow the management team that I had been working with the best chance of a smooth transition. In reality, this meant that I was committed to around five days' work a month. I had spent most of my business life to this point negotiating one thing or another and, unfortunately, you become hardened to the reality that until a deal is signed off, it doesn't really exist. So, even though I could feel and visualise this day coming, it was quite a few hours after signing the deal before it really dawned on me that my future had suddenly changed. I had been rewarded with this gift of time and so began a completely new chapter in my life. The previous 28 years of hard work had certainly paid off. That said, and for quite some time after, I quietly struggled with a sense of loss and was surprised by the vacuum it left.

Quite typically for me I soon busied myself and, with the extra time on my hands, I now had the opportunity to pursue my passion for sailing. As a first step I decided to set about qualifying as a Yachtmaster instructor and commercial skipper. I already met the criteria required to be considered, in terms of skippered sea miles, qualifications and experience. The fact was I needed a new challenge, and deep down I had real desire to share my experience and knowledge of sailing with others, plus the summer was approaching and I could hear the sea calling.

Now it was just a case of presenting myself to the governing body in order to be assessed. I was certainly a little anxious and, for the first time in many years, I was committing to being completely out of my comfort zone. Being assessed over a full five-day period, while living and working on board a yacht, would expose any chinks in my armour. The quality of the assessors was something quite extraordinary. They were at the top of their game and completely inspiring in terms of how they imparted their knowledge. Fortunately for me, all went well. Out of our group of four, three of us met the criteria and qualified as instructors. What was interesting to me was that both the other candidates that qualified were full-time servicemen, who seemed to take the whole process in their stride. Training and being tested in an unfamiliar environment were second nature to them. Ultimately, I thoroughly enjoyed the experience and soon got involved in the industry of sail training. For the next four years I dedicated around 100 days a year to training yacht skippers and their crews in the art of sailing and yacht management. The majority of courses were over a five-day period, sea based and aboard a 40-foot yacht. During this period, and on board a variety of sailing yachts, I also had the pleasure of delivering a number of leadership and team development programmes, received by business teams and university students.

Coincidently, during this period, a small group of my sailing friends asked me if I would consider skippering a Fastnet campaign.

The Story of the Fastnet Race, Part 1: *Finding My Team*

This is something they had mentioned in the past, and I had never really taken it seriously. Being aware of the commitment required, I had previously shied away. However, it was perfect timing now that I could dedicate myself to our preparation and, to be honest, I was flattered to be asked to skipper, as many of my friends were just as capable. An iconic challenge in the sailing calendar and the largest ocean race in the world, the Royal Ocean Racing Club Fastnet race is a 608-mile test of stamina and skill. It was made famous to the wider community because of its notorious reputation for offering challenging seas, which unfortunately claimed the lives of many sailors in the famous storm of 1979. The race sets off every other year from Cowes on the Isle of Wight, the home of sailing. After looping around the Fastnet Rock, just off the coast of southern Ireland, you return via the Isles of Scilly and, traditionally, you finish in the south coast harbour of Plymouth. This race has an air of unpredictability and mystique about it. Participating Fastnet skippers and their crews automatically gain a level of respect from their fellow sailors. It was certainly an exciting opportunity, and for me, as a newly validated instructor, there would be so much that I could share from the experience.

The race is limited to a fixed number of yachts so just to qualify for entry is a challenge. In order to do this, each team has to meet minimum criteria specifying safety equipment, knowledge and experience. You also need to participate in a number of qualifying training races as a crew. Even starting the race wasn't a foregone conclusion, and we took this stage seriously as a test of our mettle as a team.

I would be lying if I said I wasn't nervous. Over the years I had sailed with and skippered many different crews, but my experience was far more slanted towards cruising and making offshore passages. This challenge was about developing an amateur racing team – a very different animal. Although I had successfully skippered a number of short races and had a reputation for making quick passages, most of these lasted for no more than 24 hours. The Fastnet race was going to take anything from 120 to 140 hours to complete. If we were going to give ourselves half a chance, the team would need to be on it 24 hours a day. Despite all of this, I found I couldn't resist the challenge. How many times in my life would I get the opportunity to skipper in such a prestigious race? I said yes and, with only 10 months of preparation time, we set about putting a yacht and team together.

The first question was where we would find our vessel. Luckily, a friend of mine offered us his 25-year-old, 38-foot yacht. As a thank you, we agreed that we would equip it with a brand-new set of sails. The yacht in question was of a pedigree suitable for the campaign, but at the owners request we purchased a new set of Dacron cruising sails as opposed to high-performing laminated sails. The cruising sails would go on for many years to come whereas the laminated sails would degrade that much quicker, although they are much lighter and hold a better shape. What did this mean to our amateur racing team? A loss of no more than about 5% in our overall speed, but this translated to perhaps six or seven hours overall. However, Dacron sails are relatively bulletproof, easy to handle and less likely to be accidently damaged. Quite a consideration when you have a lot of training to do. Was I going to lay awake at night for a month after the race, contemplating what laminated sails might have done to our finishing place? Possibly!

So, we had the vessel. Now we needed a total crew of eight. Our initial group of five provided the nucleus in terms of the minimum skills required to run a successful campaign. We then set about recruiting another three. The entry criteria for our team

The Story of the Fastnet Race, Part 1: *Finding My Team*

were simple: you needed previous sailing experience at competent crew level, you had to be physically fit and available for at least 75% of the training days and, most importantly, you needed a can-do attitude and a sense of humour. In no time at all, we had our team. Unfortunately, due to a recurring injury, one member from the initial group actually had to bow out before training commenced, but he was quickly replaced. Luckily, this turn of fate only added strength to our whole campaign as the outgoing crew member volunteered to act as administrator and our shore base contact. This allowed our team members to devote their time to the practical elements of sailing.

Although our sailors had varying levels of skill and experience, the majority were coastal skippers in their own right and knew their way around a yacht. We were certainly not the youngest bunch out there, with an average age of around 50 years old, but we could draw on many hours on the sea and rich memories of successes and failures that would guide our decision-making. One had crewed in an around-the-world race, another had raced with a team across the Atlantic and others had sailed the coastal waters of the UK and various islands around the globe. So, when you consider the above, it seemed that all I had to do was bring them together. However, although I had sailed with at least half the crew before, this was mainly at different times and they had never worked together. They were a group of strong personalities with individual styles. The reality was that this was a completely scratch team, meaning we needed to learn how to function as a unit afresh. They had huge potential, but I needed to turn this into reality. It was only as we began to train out on the water together that I truly started to understand what was required for us to operate as one.

Bear in mind that, for most, sailing is a hobby and not a career, and that was true for this team. What we actually had on board was a head teacher, a structural engineer, a car mechanic, a builder, a telephone mast engineer, a property developer, an estate agent and myself. But this wasn't a disadvantage. The variety of skills they had gained in their working lives offered as much benefit to the team as their sailing prowess. In fact, most were owner managers of private companies, and this brought with it an underlying strength of character and determination which would prove invaluable during some challenging moments during our journey. Most mature business owners have faced a number of tough decisions in their careers. When time is critical, they know that avoiding or delaying a decision will likely make it worse, so they automatically look for a solution. This approach is vital in an environment where maintaining momentum is key. With the above in mind, the challenge that lie ahead was becoming more attractive to me day by day.

Chapter 1

Finding Your Leadership Framework: The High Alignment and High Autonomy Model

In this chapter, I want to explore the importance of having a strong framework for leading and managing your team. This underpins everything. We'll consider how an expert skipper would approach this and how central it is to successful team dynamics.

The skipper who is faced with a new team for the first time, especially a team that is going to embark on an offshore passage, will want to structure how the team operates and communicates on a fundamental level. They are acutely aware of the fact that any plan is governed by the collective limits of the crew. The environment they are working within is unpredictable and the stakes are high, so many measures are adopted to reduce the risks. Every member of the team has a valuable role to play in this. A small working crew is exactly that: it doesn't have room for passengers. Very successful skippers are a reflection of very capable teams.

If you are going to sea and you have been many times before, you know that a solid framework is the only way that you will sleep soundly at night. Even a small, unnoticed navigational error could at best delay your arrival and at worst take you into the rocks.

When I'm introduced to a business for the first time as an advisor, I've noticed some common themes emerge. Usually, they have either been established for some time or they are very much in the early stages of their business growth when they seek outside advice from professionals. They are normally well founded on a set of core values, have a great range of products and services, and most have a clear understanding of where they are trying to go. So, why are they asking for advice? Or, more specifically, why are they not achieving what they desire?

It may come down to the other theme that often emerges. Many of those businesses that have been successfully trading for five to 10 years have managers that barely have the time to pop their heads above the parapet. They struggle to see what the world may have to offer. They are so deeply engrossed in the daily running of the business that they cannot see the bigger picture; they cannot find the path to growth. The business is either operating at, or has reached, its natural ceiling of trading. There is a temptation to slip into what I refer to as 'busy idiot syndrome'. I have many friends and colleagues who have developed businesses like this or operate within them. They would forgive me for labelling some of them as suffering from this affliction. I am sure we can all recall times when our behaviour has warranted pinning that badge on our shirt.

However, that's not to say it's easy to remedy. It takes a well-disciplined approach, and often an investment of time and money, to step away from the daily noise of our organisations and zoom out in order to look at your department or company objectively. This is key to business and personal development. You need to see clearly where you have positioned yourself as a leader and how that may be impacting others in the organisation, as well as how that needs to develop and change. Are you constantly involved in the day-to-day activity within the team, or are you able to maintain a high level of strategic clarity? Where you position yourself as leader is fundamentally governed by two factors: the size of your organisation or team, and the competency level of those that you employ. In terms of size, I am referring to the leader's ability to distribute resources effectively. They can be constrained financially, by manpower or, as I will discuss later, they can simply be hampered by having too many subordinates to manage.

A planning tool that I often refer to, which helps leaders to position themselves for success, is the high alignment and high autonomy framework. This is described in figure 1.1 on page 11. You may have seen similar diagrams before. The truth is that these concepts are borne of well-established business theory and practice. As Stephen Bungay says in his book, *The Art of Action*: **"Things that have been mastered are forgotten. Each generation has to relearn old lessons and acquire old skills. Just apply the same principles to new situations."** To me that is a perfect statement. We need to look to others' experience and expertise to find our own path forward. This framework is built on the theory that if you could position yourself to continuously focus on the "what" within your business, as opposed to the "how" and "when", you are more likely to achieve those high-level goals that are key for overall growth and development. In practice, it is all about the timing. In order to drive true alignment, you will need to concentrate much of your efforts into developing and communicating your vision. Alignment can only be gained once the purpose is understood and agreed with the team. It then becomes a natural step for you to place more responsibility on others, who are now better informed and therefore able to autonomously make decisions, within the agreed parameters. Positioning yourself correctly adds tremendous value to your wellbeing and to those you wish to influence. Just imagine if you could go to work confidently every day in the knowledge that your team all have a common direction and are fully aligned with the goals of the business. You have the perfect recipe for successfully operating with clarity and purpose.

Of course, it's never simple. There are many components to operating a business on a daily basis, all of which have an effect on our ability to maintain our direction. But, in order to maintain our big-picture understanding of the business and its ultimate goals and not let these distractions pull us off course, it is paramount that we refer to foundational frameworks. These will help us to logically apply sound principles to everyday challenges and opportunities. The diagram on page 11 is the version that I use when I'm advising businesses. It helps them understand the direction that leaders need to take. At this stage, I have simply divided the model into four boxes, each of which describe the leader's position in relation to their team of greater or lesser alignment and autonomy. For the sake of this short summary, each main box has been titled together with a brief explanation to the meaning. But where do we start when using the diagram? Recognising where you currently are, and thus where you need to go, is key to establishing a clear path to effective leadership. Therefore, when you visualise yourself within this framework, consider how far up, down or along the scale you may be now, and what direction you are travelling in and why. You may well be just entering or leaving a box; so, for now, just consider the advantages and disadvantages of where you are and where you could go next. I recognise that, from time to time as a leader, you may find yourself in any one of these roles. It is a fact of business life that, due to certain project demands, you may have to stray from your preferred approach in order to maintain momentum and temporally support others. However, in order to develop the team and grow your organisation in the long

Chapter 1: Finding Your Leadership Framework

term, it is important to spend the majority of your time positioned correctly.

Before we delve into a brief summary of each box, it is important for me to explain the meaning of a couple of the leadership management styles that I refer to and how they are to be understood within the book. The leader-follower management style is probably the most widely practised approach and one that most people can relate to and recognise. It is based on the traditional and well-embedded model of a person in charge (leader), who then gives instruction to others (followers). This type of leader tends to recruit and develop follower types and, in extreme circumstances, could be seen as a dictator. More likely

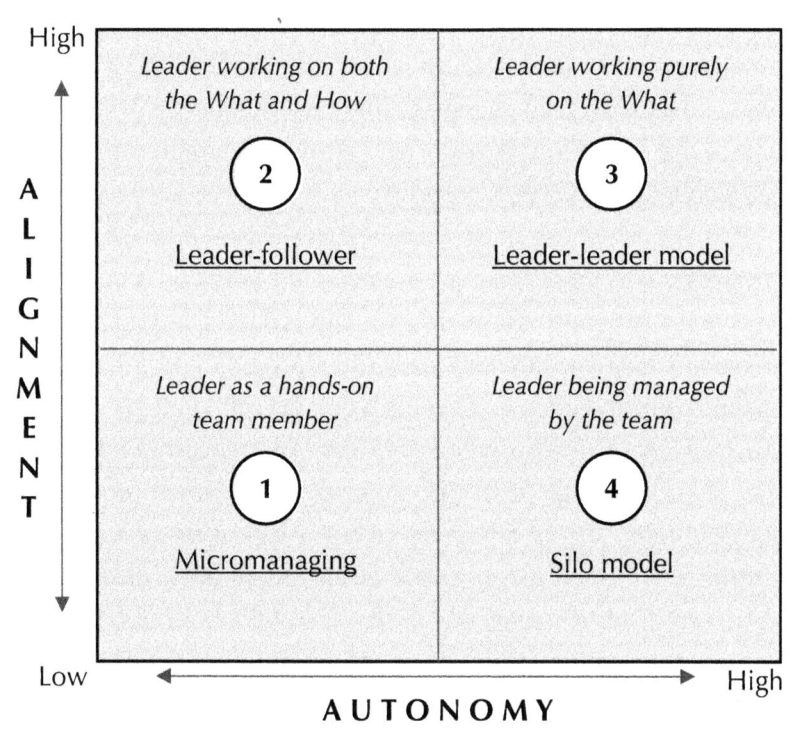

ALIGNMENT		
High	Leader working on both the What and How **(2)** Leader-follower	Leader working purely on the What **(3)** Leader-leader model
Low	Leader as a hands-on team member **(1)** Micromanaging	Leader being managed by the team **(4)** Silo model
	Low ◄──── AUTONOMY ────► High	

Figure 1.1: The high alignment, high autonomy framework

though, you will recognise this leader as someone who is successful and hardworking, but who struggles to share responsibility and to hold others truly accountable. Their teams can seem rudderless in their absence and, due to the leader's lack of trust in others, they fail to delegate, which ultimately prevents true growth. The leader-leader management style, on the other hand, looks to create high levels of both alignment and autonomy within teams. The premise in this model is to allow the organisation's vision and purpose to gain traction through supporters rather than followers. You will recognise the leader as someone who always has the bigger picture in mind. They are consistent in their approach and value the input of others. They are masters of delegation and put their trust in key players. Their preferred style is to guide and coach others in the pursuit of excellence and, ultimately, they are fully aware that scalability only comes from high alignment and high autonomy. Their teams reflect the leader's approach and are very capable of working independently with clear purpose.

Box one is where most leaders start. This is also where new businesses and those leaders who have just taken on a new team, or joined a new business, mainly sit. This is natural as you are likely to be familiarising yourself with the strengths and weaknesses of the team, in order to develop your overall strategy. Beware, however, that it is also where the less experienced control freak sits. There is a high level of hands-on management and micro-management. This is driven by either a lack of resources or, in a more established team, a lack of alignment and autonomy. In some cases, this is mainly due to the size of the business. You may be a start-up with a team of four. All of you are contributing, full time, to the income stream, and it's all hands on deck. It is as you grow from this level that the fun starts. You often see this leader struggling to effectively delegate. They are usually the last person to leave the office and the first to arrive.

Box two is typically where the leader-follower manager sits. This scenario is normally characterised by a strong and charismatic leader who has clearly aligned the team behind the business. Often, they operate through familiarity with the players. However, as a leader, they continue to have to work on both the "what" and the "how" of the business, and thus they do not empower their team to take on responsibility and have autonomy over decisions and tasks. The downside to this approach is that, as the team grows, the expanded lines of communication create confusion and the leader becomes very busy. Although some would regard these leaders as valuable assets to any business, as they appear productive, the reality is this model often reaches a natural ceiling of efficiency and will struggle to truly grow. This is also where the more mature, experienced controller type remains throughout their career. They are still a control freak, but with the experience to dampen its extremes. Many businesses and organisations operate at this level unknowingly.

Box three is the ultimate goal. The leader is able to clearly align their team with shared goals as well as give them a high level of autonomy so they can work independently. The leader is able to clearly communicate their intentions through a cascading information network. They are able to stay clearly focused on the "what", whilst guiding and coaching on the "how" and "when". This leader knows the value of recruiting competent key players and allowing them to operate freely within clearly defined boundaries and parameters. The team clearly understands the value of this approach and, in fact, they adopt and operate in a leadership style themselves, completing business objectives independently, to a high standard, whilst being fully aware of their contribution to the wider purpose of the business.

Box four is never an intentional route, but it is a by-product of ineffective leadership in all the other areas. In this box you may see businesses that have very effective departments and highly skilled managers and supervisors. However, due to the lack of true alignment, the culture becomes one of working in silos. This can lead to chaos and inefficiency within the business as a whole. An example of this is departments within the same business competing against one another in terms of their efficiency, profit contribution, etc. There is then a tendency for individuals to work for the benefit of their department only, as opposed to the overall business strategy. This silo culture is not to be confused with individuals and departments that require independence to be effective. The key to avoiding a silo culture is communication and alignment to a common purpose.

Those in box one are tempted into box four by the need and pressure to share responsibility and give autonomy away before true alignment has been achieved. Plus, an inexperienced leader can be drawn into this position purely through lack of knowledge. A good example of this is when a business leader becomes beholden to individual expertise and highly technical departments. It can be difficult for the leader to clearly articulate what is needed to fulfil the business purpose. The early days of IT departments and the modern digital world illustrated this problem, as leaders had to put themselves in the hands of others in order to progress. Constantly driving for overall alignment is key in order to avoid this pitfall.

Those in box two, in an attempt to move to box three, often slip accidentally into box four. This is often due to their underlying nature, which is drawn to the leader-follower style. They are unable

Chapter 1: Finding Your Leadership Framework

to truly embrace autonomy as a leader. In fact, they unwittingly breed a culture of silos that have individual leader-follower types. Unfortunately, in order to harmonise autonomy and alignment, the leader is forced back to box one and the micromanagement world.

The leader in box three often falls into box four when they're distracted by new opportunities or personal agendas, even if the business has been operating very effectively for a period. In this example, if the alignment and autonomy model is not brought under control quickly, you face a period of the tail wagging the dog. This can be particularly apparent for a number of misalignment issues. Here are some typical examples. When departments or businesses merge, you are automatically faced with realigning the group. It is quite natural for individuals and departments to try and protect their position, and therefore they may take an inward perspective for a period. Similarly, when working up an exit strategy for business owners, there is a risk that you may compromise alignment with key players and derail the model. When the leader themselves is approaching retirement, or simply looking to move on, a business that lacks a robust succession management plan will run the risk of reliance on others if they don't have true alignment.

We will discuss at length over the coming chapters how to stay on track towards box three and avoid the pitfalls of shifting towards the wrong path. If you want to truly elevate your position, both as a person and as a business, you need to fully embrace the leader-leader approach. There is a fundamental difference between a supporter and a follower in this context. Consider the world of politics for a moment. On the whole, supporters buy into the ethos and integrity of a party's manifesto. Even though they may have a charismatic leader, the political party knows that, if they have enough supporters aligned with their vision, the supporters themselves become the strength and driving force. Another great example of this is the world of football teams. Their supporters (fans) are not just there to follow the team. They themselves feel very much part of the organisation and play a major role in its success. In terms of the business world, the leader-leader model is about the owners and senior managers developing a culture that encourages each and every individual to adopt a leadership approach to task completion. Through good communication, the senior leaders look to the supporters (the team) to drive the business vision and purpose, allowing the leader the time to coach and guide on alternative ways to succeed, as opposed to dictating the way forward. Each individual within the leader-leader model is fully aware of the value of their contribution towards the overall purpose. They take responsibility, are accountable for their output and feel empowered by their role. Put simply, they have adopted a leader's approach.

Putting it into practice:

- Plot where you think you are on the alignment and autonomy scale in the diagram above.
- Consider each box and what they mean in practice. Draw on your own experiences to recognise the signs of leadership in these scenarios.
- Think about the other leaders in your business and where they sit on the scale.
- Contemplate what it would take to move yourself to box three.

The Story of the Fastnet Race, Part 2: *Coming Together*

Having secured a vessel and team, we were in a position to start our training proper. The race itself would require a window of around eight days in mid-August, and we needed to allow a further 15 or so days for on-the-water training and the qualifying races. Plus, a number of the crew would have to attend approved first aid and sea survival training courses. The level of commitment required in the spring and early summer was therefore pretty high, especially when you consider this wasn't their day job. This tension often added to the group dynamics. During training sessions, I could clearly see on a number of occasions that an individual wasn't really with us. As said before, many were owner managers and were often distracted by troubles back in their businesses. In fact, on one occasion, one of the senior key players in our team received a call from his office at the beginning of an offshore training weekend. As he came off the phone you could see the anxiety creeping over his face. It had just come to light that a project they had recently completed had a critical component that had been incorrectly supplied and fitted, which in turn could have caused a catastrophic disaster. This was a problem that could cost hundreds of thousands of pounds to rectify; it was potentially fatal to his business. We were all certainly distracted and concerned by this event. What did we do in response? We carried on sailing, but we stayed within mobile phone range of the shore, and this very capable and experienced businessman spent hours on his phone resolving this issue. Some 36 hours later it transpired that the component they had used was in fact of a higher grade than specified, and in the end all was okay. The whole team shared this man's emotional journey during the weekend. It was probably not our best training period, but certainly our best performance in terms of peer support.

Now it was time to focus the whole team and their alignment as a group, all the time knowing there were going to be big gaps between training weekends. It was critical that I established a clear purpose that they could all align with. My overriding goal was to complete the race (many don't) and bring the team back as one. Plus, of course, keeping them free from personal injury, both physically and in terms of their spirit and team morale. This was a big race and something we all wanted to experience. Although we were clearly in a position to compete competently, we knew the top half of the fleet were far out of our reach. However, we could certainly have the second half of the fleet firmly within our sights. Those teams were far more likely to have similar set ups to our own: an amateur scratch team in an unfamiliar boat with an experienced skipper. Therefore, my secondary goal was to finish as far up the second half of the fleet as possible. We set a bold target to finish in the top 200 yachts overall, out of the 325 entries.

It's important to understand that our goal wasn't established and agreed from the outset, as this would have been an extremely hard sell to the team. At this early stage, there was a high risk of overestimating the team's ability. Initially all I had to go on was their enthusiasm and a vague understanding of their individual skill level, but the success of this campaign hinged on a complete team performance. I needed to gain their full trust before predicting our capabilities. The easiest way to do this was to get out on the water and work with each individual, first sailing a mile in their deck shoes and seeing the sailing world from their perspective, before offering my own take. If viewed from afar, those first couple of training weekends and the first qualifying race were not very pretty. These were all good sailors, and most of them could skipper a yacht safely and get themselves and their crew from A to B. What was clear, however, is that most had operated as leader-follower captains of their ships and were inclined to give instruction for others to follow. Their communication skills were certainly interesting and widely varied, and why not? We all have our own unique way of expressing our opinions, and those opinions were ultimately contributing towards our strategic thinking. What was lacking in these early training sessions was a better understanding of everybody's capabilities and their true strengths. It wasn't just me that had to work out where each player would be best placed in the team. I could clearly sense that this was a concern for every member of the group. One thing was for sure. In order to develop trust and respect across the team, I needed to structure my communication in such a way that it was always received as valued and appropriate, but also challenging, in order to expose the best way forward for us as a whole. This is a conundrum for all leaders when blending capable individuals into a new team. Sailing can be quite a competitive environment, and over the years I have noticed that many skippers and boat owners avoid sailing with those that might know a little more than them. It's a way of retaining the upper hand, even if they're nominally putting their guest in the position of leader. It's quite a challenging and potentially stressful environment for the man or woman in charge, particularly with someone watching over them. Going to sea with two captains or, in this case, possibly four or five, could have been quite entertaining for an observer. How was

I going to manage the personal expectations and the pride of each individual, whilst balancing that against what was ultimately best for the team and our goal?

For us to be successful, I needed to develop a strong level of autonomy within the team, something that could only be gained after complete alignment on our goals and purpose. Those first couple of training sessions really highlighted the chaos caused by allowing skilled and strong characters to operate in silos. This was demonstrated on board like this. There were three main facets to running the boat: the navigation and strategy (the tacticians); the helming of the boat (the person steering); and the sail trimmers who set and adjusted the sails (the engine room). In order for this to work successfully, each and every facet has to be in harmony with one another. That probably sounds obvious, but it's not always acknowledged. It only works if each area is aware of what the others are doing. Now, imagine spending 48 hours with seven other men or women in a living space smaller than the average lounge, where you all eat, sleep and work. Plus, you all share only one bathroom facility. Add to that the potentially harsh and unforgiving environment of the sea, winds and tides, with your home spending much of the time at an angle of 20°, and you have the recipe for high levels of sleep deprivation. The reality in those first couple of training sessions was that individual experience and sometimes tiredness influenced the behaviour of each person, and if they felt something needed adjusting or altering, they would often carry out a task in isolation. Though convinced that what they were doing was right, they often failed to communicate their intentions and actions to others. Sometimes, and especially for this new amateur team, subtle tweaks would go unnoticed for quite a period, until another facet of the boat began to struggle to maintain its position. Without going into the real detail of how a particular action in one area of a yacht has a knock-on effect in another, this silo approach is probably best summed up like this: it's rather like having the manufacturing arm of your business efficiently producing much more product than is required by the sales team. The manufacturing department are chuffed with their performance, but because they failed to communicate their intentions they are not in sync with the rest of the business. In terms of sailing, my experience tells me that extended time at sea has a habit of bringing out both the best and worst in one's character. Allowing problems to develop through lack of communication and not having a common goal to keep us on the right track was simply not an option.

We were going to be testing ourselves in a number of these 48-hour training sessions, most of which included a period of downtime and a well-earned beer ashore. It seemed clear to me and a couple of others that we'd never really be able to judge how 130 hours at sea would affect each team member. This was something we'd only discover in the race itself. This realisation helped to focus all of our energies and future training towards simulating a typical day in the race. Where this varied from before is that we would run the boat and systems as if we were at sea for a number of days, as opposed to having breaks ashore during training. In a typical 24-hour qualifying race from an English port to a French port, we would race to the finishing line and immediately turn around and sail back, without stopping in France, in order to extend the continuous time at sea. Plus, we would add in various scenarios on the way back, such as simulating a man overboard recovery at night and extra sail changes in difficult sea conditions. This approach helped us to gain a valuable insight into how individuals and the team fared during extended times at sea. This was a style that I was used to from my own training days as a Navy reservist.

It was also a valuable lesson I'd learnt from a casual conversation with a sailing school principal a few years earlier. My eldest son, Robert, had a desire to compete in the Fastnet race when he was only 16. He found himself a position on a scratch team being put together at a sailing school in the Hamble, near Southampton. In fact, this school had two identical yachts and had managed to fill both boats with new crews, each led by an experienced in-house skipper. One day, when waiting on the quayside for Rob to return from a qualifying race, I commented to the school's principal that Rob's team was doing rather well in the qualifying races against the school's other boat. He made an interesting distinction between the two skippers which stuck with me. He said that Rob's young and inexperienced skipper was technically the better racing sailor out of the two and could stay focused in these short 24-hour races. The other skipper, in contrast, was a far more experienced hand and knew that, during these qualifying races, he had to focus on preparing the crew for a race that was likely to take five full days at sea. He was training his team to take charge and assume responsibility for the yacht whilst he was asleep and off watch rather than worrying about their results against the other boat. The school principal had it absolutely right. The younger and more inexperienced skipper had to rely far more on himself during that five-day race because, as he hadn't looked at the bigger picture, he failed to focus on developing his team. The end result was that the more prepared team came home first when it counted. Nobody remembers where you finished in the qualifiers, however much you might like to remind them.

With this firmly in my mind, I briefed the team and aligned them all with the idea that we would raise the stakes and treat each training session as a typical day in the race. Asking mature individuals to train in this make-believe manner is a similar challenge to that of asking your senior work colleagues to participate in role play. Volunteers are never forthcoming. However, in the world of professional sport and in all of the emergency and armed services, they recognise the value of simulated training. So, as the leader of this group, it was my job to sell the advantages of this proven method.

The first two training sessions had built up my trust and influence within the group. I had patiently spent quality time with them, observed their abilities and began to understand their strengths and weaknesses. I avoided being overly critical and offered only snippets of advice and guidance. This had gone some way towards breaking down barriers. I could feel them opening their minds to a new way of operating, and a good level of respect was developing. Sometimes it can be really difficult for those already comfortable with their level of understanding to value training. Plus, fears can get in the way of the process because people withdraw from difficult learning situations. Individual fears present themselves in a number of ways, and as a good coach you learn to recognise when fear is present and to how it may be impacting someone's behaviour. Helping others to face this, especially as part of a team, can be very rewarding. However, it does require understanding and a high level of communication skills. In the wrong hands and delivered at the wrong level, training can be seen as teaching your grandmother to suck eggs. You need to recognise the reluctance in some to receive learning, especially when they are long in the tooth. However, if you can offer insights pitched and delivered at the right level, most people enjoy the experience and are better for it. When training is at a high level, I look to shared learning as my preferred route, where both the leader and the team work together, sharing their knowledge and skills and debating and testing various approaches. This is an open approach to learning and takes advantage of your shared goal. It also works very well in helping individuals to discuss their fears. You can enhance this further by bringing experts in from the outside, to offer further insights into specialist subjects. With the above in mind, and although we now had a good working relationship, my next tactic was what really made the difference. I decided to seek out expert guidance to help us get to the next level. This ended up being an invaluable tactic which brought us together, allowed us to grow and gave needed credence to my "practice makes perfect" mantra. To set the scene, I and another member of the team went along to a casual evening bringing together new Fastnet skippers. There were two guest speakers: both were skippers who had experienced the Fastnet at its worst in the 1979 campaign. Over a few beers we had an evening of storytelling, and the value of that night has stayed with me forever. I was able to blend their experience with my own and truly expand my understanding of sailing. Gaining an insight into the various survival tactics that these skippers had deployed in such a violent storm was invaluable, and a deep reminder to expect the unexpected. One skipper graphically explained how their biggest problem was surfing uncontrollably down the face of these mountainous waves, to only then get stuck in the bottom of a trough waiting for the next wave to crash violently upon them. He explained that, after a period of being in the lap of the gods, they devised a tactic of sailing the yacht across each wave as opposed to being picked up by it and driven straight down its face. This strategy slowed the yacht's progress and prevented it from slamming into the trough at the bottom, allowing them to reduce the chances of capsizing. They gave lots of technical advice and practical tips to explain their solution. The competitors in 1979 were subjected to a storm lasting many hours that produced waves in excess of 60 feet high, driven by winds of 90mph. As a sailor, you hope you will never have to employ your own tactics to deal with such a scenario, and it's certainly difficult to simulate any training that could ever fully prepare you for such an extreme situation. Therefore, listening to those that have had first-hand experience is vital if you want to give yourself the best chance of succeeding. To this day, I very rarely turn down an opportunity to listen to quality stories from experts and, on the flip side, I tend to give a wide berth to those that fail to walk the talk.

Buoyed by this experience, and aiming to raise the bar at our next weekend training session, I invited one of the guest speakers to join us for a day. He was actually the tutor and instructor on my Yachtmaster shore-based theory course many years before. As well as being a Fastnet veteran, he had an abundance of skippering experience. Over the years, however confident I am of my own ability to develop and lead teams, I have always tapped into the knowledge of experts in order to continually grow, and this was the perfect opportunity. On board our yacht, I was deemed the expert but, by bringing along my own guru, I was able to demonstrate the approach that I wished to adopt regarding shared learning. Throughout our first day, the team went through a number of drills and simulations. They would witness me talking through my plan with the guru prior to starting, then they would see me almost narrate each move out loud, just before I was about to make a decision. This is a teaching and communication strategy that I had used many times before and an approach I use when skippering. I often refer to it as thinking out loud. It has a twofold effect. Firstly, it helps the narrator to consider what they are doing, as having to say it out loud makes it a clear declaration of intent as opposed to an independent thought. The second benefit is that those in the vicinity do not have to read your mind and, should your proposed action have potentially dire consequences, there is an opportunity for others to interject. When training, you often want others to learn from their mistakes, therefore you would only interject if the likely outcome was deemed as dangerous. This is a communication style that the whole team needed to practice when carrying out critical tasks. We also adopted the 'brief and back brief' approach, which is an integral part of communication for teamwork. Any task requiring a brief by a leader is considered by those who are responsible for carrying out the task. They then back brief the leader with their proposed plan in order to establish clear alignment. I find this approach invaluable when I am skippering a yacht as it ensures nothing is lost in translation. A good example is if the task requires two people to go forwards to the bow of a yacht at night on a noisy sea. As long as you have had a clear back brief, you can relax in the knowledge that the team have a plan and understand the outcome required. I have witnessed many an inexperienced skipper in this context who has set a brief for a task, asked the crew if they understood it and then sent them forward. Often, due to the darkness and noise, the skipper, who is normally safely in the cockpit of the yacht nearer to the back of the boat, spends the next hour shouting instruction at the crew on how to do it. The crew, only hearing every third word, eventually end up returning to the cockpit and asking: "What did you say?" Surprising as it might be, the whole thing often starts again without a back brief, and what should have taken half an hour takes a least twice as long. To avoid this happening throughout the training weekend, all our intended actions and plans were spoken out loud, so the guru didn't need to second guess our thoughts. He was free to continually observe the whole team without the need to didactically lead or question us, leading to a much freer and more positive learning environment. A good day was had by all, and when we went ashore for a meal that night, the conversation was lively and much more open. Indeed, self-critiquing was apparent. The process of shared learning had successfully got the team talking. It had created a safe environment (non-competitive and non-judgemental) for each and every person to express, practice and test both their own and others' ways of doing things.

Chapter 2

What's Driving Your Business – People or Process?

The 24/7 nature of passage making at sea forces the leader to rely on others in order to be truly successful. That inherent reliance is why a good skipper will devote a lot of time to selection and training of their crew. They are acutely aware that, once the passage plan is in place and the lines are slipped from the shore, the goal is shared and ultimate success is in the hands of the crew and their ability to assess and manage the unknowns as they appear. Although systems and processes are essential to maintain order, it's the people on board who will have the biggest influence when shaping and adapting the course required to stay on track and arrive at the chosen destination. The skipper will rely on their experience and knowledge to suggest what actions are required in the crux moments.

As the stakes at sea are often high, placing your crew members in the wrong position could result in catastrophic failure, where both lives and the vessel could be at risk. This could be as simple as promoting someone to a position of responsibility before they are truly ready or failing to understand where the real strength of an individual lies. The skipper naturally attempts to balance experience amongst the team and will focus on discipline and thoroughness during the passage. This assesses whether the selection process is robust and if training and development is being delivered at the right level.

So, what does this tell us? We must look to our people first as the drivers of success in our businesses, and we must make sure that we place them in the right position for them to reach their potential and satisfy these high expectations. However, the reality is often very different. Business leaders, and especially owner managers, striving to improve their efficiency and hit their targets, seem to be on a constant cycle of either: paying for high quality management who strive to keep them on track; or implementing elaborate systems and processes supported by administrators who attempt to marshal the business. Indeed, the scientific method of management endorses the latter, promising to improve productivity by analysing and synthesising workflows and turning employees into virtual robots, monitored by armies of supervisors. But management and process solutions cannot win the day on their own; without the careful development of a well-constructed team, we are doomed to failure. This manager often lives in a world of frustration, never really stepping back to truly understand the composition of the team and positioning of individuals or dedicating the time to evaluate the impact of their competency level.

In fact, the well-constructed team drives good systems and procedures. Their success is all about the human interface at each level. Energy and momentum come from the operator. Those that take true ownership and are skilled at their job understand that, if left in the wrong hands, most systems will eventually fail. If it is a critical tool, then it must be managed by the most competent of individuals. A simple guide on how to run a system can work well, but the level of output will ultimately be influenced by the experience and motivation of the person who uses it. It requires experience to challenge the quality of the input and skill to control and measure the quality of the output. For example, imagine handing a set of ingredients and a recipe to a novice cook. You'd likely have a different outcome in terms of quality compared to handing the exact same information to an experienced chef. Even though on paper they both have the same system to follow, the benefits of aptitude and experience will no doubt affect the end result.

A good example of this is management accounts. They can be of huge value to those able to utilise their experience and understanding. I have witnessed numerous senior individuals having their lives driven by what the numbers have reported as opposed to how they can *influence* the numbers. Every act of recording data about a business is an opportunity to learn more. The information gives a wise manager an indication of the actions required to improve both the immediate performance and subsequent outcomes. They are able to interpret and analyse; gathering insight to shape strategy. It is all about operating ahead of the plan.

Success in a team is all about its composition and the competency level of each individual appointed. It seems that businesses have difficulty placing the right people in the right position. Typically, you can see this in departments and organisations whose managers seem to be constantly fighting fires and are struggling to truly identify the strengths within their team. It takes leadership to have the confidence to not compromise on the choice of employee for a particular role, even if that takes time and expense. I understand that it is often hard to press the stop button and come away from the everyday activities of business. However, in terms of personnel, it is vital that you assess where you are and what it is you need. It is a leader's role to identify the strengths and weaknesses of group members and select the best candidate for the required task. If undervalued, this basic level of resource management could undermine the entire performance of the team, leading to an unhealthy cycle of frustration. As mentioned earlier, the stakes are often higher for the skipper, where the crew's lives could be at risk, as opposed to the business manager. That said, even in the world of business, the impact of failure on the welfare of all employees should not be underestimated.

As a leader, the earlier you embrace the fact that it is people that drive your business and not process, the sooner you will be in a position to fully align your teams and develop the ultimate leader-leader business model.

Putting it into practice:

- Take a good look at how your business or team is being driven. Is it by process or people?
- How much time is spent by your business and its leaders on reacting to historical reports, compared to evaluating live information?
- Consider your critical processes, and evaluate who is monitoring and critiquing the input.
- How good are the individuals in your team? Are you completely familiar with their strengths and weaknesses?
- Reflect on the people who make up your business, and look to how you can put talent first.

Chapter 3
The Art of Leadership: Building Trust and Cohesion

Before we talk any further about the team, let's have a look at the role of leader. It is worth reflecting on how good a leader you are, whether you're positioned correctly and what type of leaders your business really needs. Is there such a thing as a born leader, or is it another skill that can be learnt through practice and experience? Personally, I believe it is a combination of both. There are certainly young individuals that I have met and worked with that, despite their lack of experience, have the attributes and behavioural traits that would suit directing and guiding others. Many of the armed services around the world have a long and successful history of identifying and recruiting potential leaders, suggesting that the aptitude is there from an early age. They are then put through rigorous accelerated training programmes to enable them to be truly effective leaders. The same can be said in sport when, again, exposure to a high level of structured training can nurture bright young minds that seem capable of effectively leading others. The business world doesn't offer as many opportunities for individuals to experience such intense training methods. I recognise that each discipline has its own unique variances and you cannot necessarily train all leaders in the same way. It is also interesting to note the number of leaders who were effective in their chosen field of expertise who have subsequently failed when they tried to take their skills to a new arena. There are many stories of highly-trained servicemen and servicewomen and leading sportspeople who have paid the price for stepping into the world of business. However, there are just as many who have had great success. This suggests there are common principles, traits and behaviours that can be drawn from these examples that, if understood and practised, offer leaders a real opportunity to succeed. The key is understanding how leadership skills will translate across fields and how they may have to evolve and adapt to a different context. Let's look at an example.

A retired Royal Navy officer once told me the story of when he left the services and decided to buy a local shop in a country village. He knew it would be a huge step away from where he once was, but he felt that it would be very satisfying to work alongside his wife serving a small village community. In their mid-50s, both he and his wife still had plenty of energy and enthusiasm, which in hindsight turned out to be very handy. His attempts at managing and motivating the local paperboys and papergirls, using the same direct, no-nonsense officers' approach he had in the Navy, completely failed. After only a few months at the helm, this retired lieutenant commander was the only paperboy left in the village. He had successfully provoked his first ever mutiny and all his employees had left, fed up with his authoritarian manner. One morning, sitting on a garden wall at the crack of dawn, with paper delivery sacks over each shoulder, he reflected on where it had all gone wrong. Fortunately for him, later that morning he was thumbing through one of the papers and noticed an advert for a naval training centre that was looking to recruit retired officers to support their programme. He couldn't get back quickly enough. This is a classic example of a man that would have been regarded by his peers as an excellent and highly-trained leader. However, when it came to communicating at a grassroots level, he had simply

Chapter 3: The Art of Leadership: Building Trust and Cohesion

failed to understand that civvy street plays by different rules, and your average cheeky young paperboy didn't give two hoots if you had captained the *Ark Royal*. I had the pleasure of going to sea with this officer, and he certainly knew how to motivate his team. What was missing in the world of his village store was simply the layered structure of leaders that he had grown to rely upon for support. His instructions were going directly to the coalface when, in the past, through the typical leader-leader approach, with a cascading order of command, this man's requests would have been rephrased and packaged in a language that each level could relate to. Some great leaders are able to communicate at all levels at a flick of a switch, but many correctly rely on others who have the autonomy to carry out instructions as they see fit, with a common goal in mind.

So, what attributes do we need to be effective leaders? How do you create highly-aligned teams and allow them to work in a business with the autonomy to freely operate within clear boundaries? How do you avoid your leadership style limiting the growth of those around you or, alternatively, promoting members of your team to leadership roles before they are ready? As discussed earlier, there is a real danger of giving over autonomy before alignment has been truly established. But, in order to create alignment – to progress and grow as a unit – you need to build solid layers of communication and create a leadership culture that is recognised by all. It's all about finding that balance.

As an avid observer of people, I have always been fascinated by the correlation between how people operate in their personal and professional lives. What type of friend are you? Are you a good parent, son or daughter? Do you naturally put the welfare of others before your own? Often, someone who is considerate in their personal life is considerate in their working life, and I think this is one of the cornerstones of effective leadership.

Often, in the workplace, we are forced into working with people that, in our private lives, we may choose not to associate with. Considerate and skilled leaders, however, have a knack of developing high levels of trust with their direct team and thus productive relationships that heal these differences. If you are a well-balanced and trusted friend, parent, son or daughter, you are more likely to adopt this style with those that you rely on in business. You must be able to see the world through the eyes of those you wish to motivate and direct, building deep understanding and mutual respect. This means spending time with your team and getting to know them on a personal level. Moreover, good leaders tend to attract and recruit like-minded team members, which leads to a naturally more cohesive group of individuals. The challenge is in trying to maintain this approach as the team size grows. While they're of a manageable size, it is relatively easy to take a genuine interest in the wellbeing of each of your players but, as a team becomes unwieldy, it's hard to remain up to date with each individual and their particular needs and struggles. As the skipper on a yacht, it is important to spend social time with the crew. This goes beyond the simple tradition of sharing a beverage ashore together. These times are valuable for getting to know who your team really are, how they tick and what motivates them outside the world you normally see them in. Taking time out to listen to others in these moments shows a side of yourself that others will respect and value. They know that, as a good leader, it will be business as usual as soon as you step back on board, but they also know that your interest in them goes beyond the work they do for you, and this helps to underpin their trust.

It is interesting that businesses throughout the world invest billions studying the behaviour traits of their clients and potential customers. And yet, when it comes to a leader understanding

Chapter 3: The Art of Leadership: Building Trust and Cohesion

their own team, many fail to appreciate the value of investing even half an hour of their own time, outside the business, to learn more about the individuals who are at the heart of their companies. Some managers believe that a work-based social activity involving the team somehow ticks the box. However, if you really want to develop those key players who respect and trust your direction, you need to invest unscheduled time with them on a personal basis, outside the daily noise of the business, simply taking a genuine interest in them. This is not something that has to happen weekly or monthly, but it is something that you must actively seek to do from time to time. The rewards easily justify such a small investment of your time. If it is not something you regularly practise now, you may well be surprised by how quickly loyalty can grow within a team that feel better connected to their leader. Many times, I have witnessed the cost to a business of a disruptive team member who can quickly unsettle the ship. So often it could have been completely avoided if a trust-based relationship had been carefully built and the leader had taken the time to have a personal chat with them outside of work to bring about a better and more enlightened mutual understanding. Good leaders know how and when it is healthy to drop their guard and allow the team to see a little more of who they are.

As a considerate leader, there are times when we need to carry someone in the team. It is what good, trusting teams do. Any one of us may need support at some point. However, when a leader makes a conscious decision to be charitable to the needs of a member of the team, they have to recognise that, in reality, it is the other team members who normally pay the price for such a decision and pick up the additional workload. This is all well and good in highly-aligned teams who recognise the value of supporting others in exceptional circumstances. The danger comes when the support required is due to the continued underperformance of a team member. Addressing that early, at a leadership level, is key if you want to maintain a high level of trust with the team as a whole. If, in fact, you are carrying a passenger who consistently fails to contribute, you need to have the courage to move them into an area better suited to their skills, or it may simply be time to move on without them.

I firmly believe that it is beneficial as a leader to limit the amount of people you directly influence, as numerous lines of communication can dilute the value of your vision. It therefore follows that those other key players who drive your business forwards should also limit the number of people they can directly influence. The leader-leader model develops a cascading information network which is far more efficient, with every individual adopting a leadership approach to each task. Along the way, you need to have the discipline to avoid micromanagement and allow skilled individuals a healthy level of interpretation, all in the pursuit of a common goal. Ultimately this leadership model empowers each and every individual to make a positive contribution to the cause, all based on a unified understanding (alignment) and a level of control (autonomy) that is set within clear parameters.

Figure 3.1 below illustrates the value of a simple and effective communications network with a leader-leader approach which limits the number of team members that each leader directs.

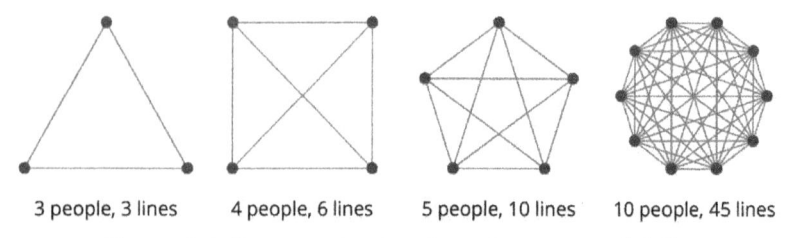

3 people, 3 lines   4 people, 6 lines   5 people, 10 lines   10 people, 45 lines

Figure 3.1 Communication lines for teams of different sizes

Chapter 3: The Art of Leadership: Building Trust and Cohesion

Now imagine the leader as one point in these diagrams, managing and orchestrating the communication lines of the team. In a team of three, four or even five, communication and management is straightforward and manageable. Managing a team of 10 with 45 lines of communication could be absolutely fine when the workload is relatively repetitive, as in a factory process. However, if your team is made up of individuals with a diverse level of skills, who each specialise in dealing with complex and bespoke projects, such as a design team, the load on the leader will be far greater. If the leader is inexperienced, you can very quickly see that a superhuman effort may be required to keep a team on track. As an individual, moreover, if you rely on the leader-follower model, you get into serious trouble as the team grows, especially if the work is of a highly technical nature. Ultimately, the business can become dangerously dependant on a few overworked leaders and individual team members won't be able to access the support and guidance they need to do a good job.

So, what makes a great leader? Standing up as the CEO of your organisation and presenting to the wider business may mean you are a great communicator, but it doesn't necessarily mean you have the skill to guide and nurture a team. However, the CEO in charge of a direct team of five or six individuals who are totally aligned in purpose and direction, through mutual trust and understanding, is likely to be a great leader. This type of leader allows their team to get on with the job in hand. They are there to guide and coach at the appropriate time and will avoid, at all costs, undermining those they rely on.

Putting it into practice:

- Consider your leadership network. Can each leader successfully influence all of their direct reports? Do they really know their team members?
- How familiar are you with your direct team? Can you see their role through their eyes?
- How often do you spend social time with your direct team?
- How can you enhance the communication network while maintaining clarity of purpose?
- Consider the size of your direct team and the number of communication lines.

The Story of the Fastnet Race, Part 3: *Working as One*

Our collective experiences were bringing us together and adding gravitas to our campaign, whether it was the evening of Fastnet storytelling, having the guru on board for a day, or just simply the improved communication. I had demonstrated my willingness to reveal my shortcomings to a sailing guru in articulating my decisions during practice, and thus I set an example of what we could achieve if we were open to learning. I could now sense a willingness in the team when practising to think out loud without the fear of saying something wrong. This proved to be critical in developing trust and respect as we continued with our training.

The next qualifying race was soon upon us. Following on from the successful day's training with the guru, it was my job the next day to consolidate this approach. It was all about communication. We would now adopt the thinking out loud tactic to basic tasks, which would underpin our approach to shared learning. The 'brief and back brief' technique would be used for communicating critical tasks. I selected one of the team members to act as the primary navigator, a senior role that is required to support the skipper's own navigational duties during the race itself. The navigator also doubled up as the skipper's number two. In order to simulate the bigger race, I needed to introduce additional levels of leadership, and I was determined to operate with a disciplined watch system. The significance of this is fundamental when sailing.

SHIPSHAPE

With extended time at sea, and when operating 24 hours a day, you require a shift system in order to man the yacht. This allows the off-watch team time to eat, rest and sleep. I prepared the team for the fact that both myself and the senior navigator were going to decide the watch structure and choose two people to act as watch leaders. Each watch would consist of three people including the watch leader. Both myself and the senior navigator would remain outside of the watch system. We would work together to ensure one of us was available to assist when more hands were needed on deck. In addition, we could each cover the navigating tasks whilst the other was asleep. The plan was to adopt this set up for the remainder of the campaign. This was a significant step towards the high alignment and high autonomy model, allowing the leader to concentrate more on the "what". By handing out specific roles and schedules to each crew member, they were able to take sole responsibility for certain tasks and work on the "how" far more independently. I had moved from a team that loosely operated under my leadership with an aligned overall purpose, to a team that would enact the strategic plan with a good level of autonomy, without the need for constant direction.

One of the less experienced crew members couldn't make this qualifying race, so for this particular weekend I was able to invite my eldest son on board. At the time Rob had not only competed in a previous Fastnet campaign, but was also a very capable young sailor and instructor. We were now roughly halfway through our allocated training days, and this was when we really needed to embed the learning. I have learnt, both at work and at sea, that it's very difficult for proud, hardworking and slightly competitive individuals to truly share their shortcomings. Many have developed strategies to avoid being so exposed. Running your own business is one of them; skippering your own yacht is certainly another.

However, it is those that challenge themselves, by exposing their knowledge and principles to their peer group, that are more likely to grow and develop into rounded individuals. I had now created the environment that made it safe to do exactly that.

The objective was simple: to always keep the boat going as quickly as possible, 24 hours a day, moving in the right direction, all whilst considering the end goal. However, it was pointless to push so hard that you damaged your crew or yacht and failed to complete. I introduced my son, Rob, to the team and said that, alongside me, he would help with answering technical questions. I reminded the whole crew that our overall training strategy for this qualifying race would be one of improved communication, putting into practice what we had recently learnt. I then briefed each watch leader and the senior navigator on the specifics of what we were trying to achieve. Plus, I asked them to independently brief their small teams and come back to me with a clear back brief and any questions. This was the first time we were able to adopt this more formal approach of briefing on objectives, supported by watch leaders. My experience told me that, if we had attempted this any sooner, it would have certainly been autonomy without alignment on goals, and that would have been disastrous. You may recall from reference to the high alignment and high autonomy framework earlier in the book that, the silo model is underpinned by giving autonomy without first establishing alignment. It can be a hard place to move from, and often you are drawn into micromanaging before you can establish true alignment. I certainly didn't have time to go on that journey. Plus, the added advantage of taking our time to select the watch leaders was that, during the earlier training sessions, each individual could clearly see the strengths within the team and completely supported the choices made.

SHIPSHAPE

Establishing agreed communication styles was key in supporting our endeavours to share knowledge, as well as being a vital component in terms of understanding someone's intention. The following is an example of why we needed to understand the intention of others before an action was taken. Unlike short distance racing around buoys, when sailing long distances there is less tweaking of the rig. Even when participating in 24-hour passages, it's not uncommon to remain on the same tack for many hours. This lack of positive action can put some skippers on edge, and they tend to constantly fiddle with the kit out of habit. All this is fine, if it suits the purpose of going quickly in the right direction. However, when observing others, I have often found this interference results in a pattern of peaks and troughs. I'm sure you all have a control freak within your organisation that simply can't help themselves but constantly interfere. I adopted a simple strategy on board that would address this problem. You may recall my earlier comment about how an action completed in isolation in one area can have a detrimental reaction in another. Therefore, once an action was planned, whoever was the team leader for the task, including myself, would have to justify and explain to their direct team any tweak they were proposing. We had all agreed that any bystander could challenge your suggestion and how you expected it would be of benefit. The added advantage of this approach was that at night, when the stakes are higher, someone wouldn't independently or accidentally do something that might endanger them or someone else.

Let's take a basic example of how this would play out. A watch leader would call for a small ease of the mainsail. If no explanation was given for the change, the crew member who was about to carry out the task would ask for the "why". The team leader would give his reason, and the task would go ahead. This simple approach hadn't featured in earlier training sessions. What happened next was much more interesting. As well as questioning the change, the team on watch would now consider what happened following the change. The team leader and crew members would monitor the result and see if the judgement was accurate. Where required, they would check this with the navigator to see that it all added up. If not, they would simply think and act again, often seeking advice and guidance from others. We had now created the ultimate learning hub. This didn't mean the crew were going to become a first-class racing team in a number of days, but it did mean that we began to iron out the extreme peaks and troughs. And the peaks and troughs had an impact. In the Fastnet race, being one minute quicker or slower every hour than the rest of the fleet could gain or lose us up to 50 places. Our small improvements could make a big difference.

During this qualifying race I could see a stark difference in our performance. This simple communication method was aligning the team further, and respect and understanding for one another was now continually growing. I now had the early signs of a team that had layers of leadership and clear levels of autonomy, driven by the watch leaders who were completely aligned with the overall goal. From now on, the remaining training sessions would adopt this approach. It had taken us some time together to get the traction we needed. I could now focus my time on coaching where it would add the most value. The overall team dynamics and leadership framework were in place and, seemingly, worked well. Our overall goal remained the same, but now we had a real chance as a unit to fulfil our ambitions.

Chapter 4

Recruiting the Right People

As you can see from earlier chapters, when planning a passage at sea, crew competency plays a major role in determining the strategy. When you inherit a crew, as opposed to selecting them, you have to appraise their capabilities as soon as possible in order to work up your plan. When handpicking a crew, you can expedite the process and be ready to go that much earlier. The world of passage making in a sailing yacht requires a 24-hour working day, and this influences your approach to planning. You need to balance the skill level within your team in order that the yacht's performance is maximised each and every hour of the day. I have found that, unless I have handpicked my team, I have needed to devote more time to correlate the team dynamics with my plan. This ensures a far greater chance of success, rather than putting the destination and passage plan before the people.

Taking the same approach to the world of business made perfect sense. By considering what I'd need for my crew to collaborate efficiently for 24 hours a day, I developed teams that could operate for long periods independently. I have participated in many planning meetings, and there is always a strong focus on 'selling' the plan to others in order to gain strong alignment. I'm an advocate of that approach, but it seems to me that much less effort is made in determining exactly how the "who" will impact the end result. We will talk much more about strategic planning later, but for now we will focus on the "who".

Recruitment is the fine art of selection. Many businesses use the services of experts to filter their candidates. This has many benefits in terms of throwing your net wider and making more efficient use of your time. It does, however, often come at a high cost and, in my experience, only really works when you and the recruiter invest quality time in understanding exactly what it is you are trying to achieve. If you are looking to recruit directly, then you need to consider your approach. When filtering through résumés, credentials are key to understanding the overall qualifications and experience of an individual. However, to determine how a candidate has actually applied each of their skills in their working life is much more difficult to gauge. The language used is so often generic gobbledygook, and the reader simply has no real clue to the individual's true experience or potential.

I have read hundreds of résumés in my time and, over the last 15 years or so, it has become more and more challenging in terms of cutting through the language used. This has driven me to adopt the approach of interviewing many more people so that I can assess them first-hand. I usually start with a simple phone conversation, to gain more of an insight to the person's character, and then I will dedicate a morning every day for a week to first interviews. By the time I have completed second interviews, I would have invested up to 30 hours of face-to-face time in order to gain one new team member. This may seem like a lot, but it pays off in the long run. You need to see it as a selection process rather than a recruitment exercise. There's a subtle difference in meaning: it is not about enlisting people; it is about carefully choosing the right candidate. You are never going to get it a hundred percent right all of the time, but the ultimate price you pay for hiring the wrong person, in terms of cost, time and disruption to other team members, is simply too high. I have noticed that those who neglect to invest their time in securing the right people for their team are exactly the same individuals who fail to invest time into developing new team members. This type of wastage, at any leadership level, is unacceptable and often reflects back the short-sightedness of the leader. When you look at staff turnover numbers, it is often the same department heads or team leaders that regularly struggle to retain staff. They will give you all sorts of reasons for their retention problems, but it is important to step back and look at the patterns. This type of management can be a by-product of a leader having too many team members. The manager is constrained by time and is in need of more help, hence the recruitment. Yet they fail to invest enough time and thought into the selection process. Ultimately, they hire just to fill an immediate need, without truly understanding the competency level of the new recruit. It simply becomes a vicious circle, one that needs stopping dead in its tracks. Ultimately, it is wise to consider that a leader who consistently has a problem with their team is in fact themselves the problem.

At the recruitment stage there often seems to be too much emphasis on the role level or type, which for some reason seems to set an expectation regarding how much time you should invest to fill a vacancy. For example, a leader may spend three months recruiting a new head of marketing but only want to spend half that time recruiting a marketing assistant, as they place less importance on the latter. In fact, every new opportunity you have in your team needs to be filled by the best person you can find and afford. Talent comes in all shapes and sizes and is required at every level. Each new employee has the potential to become a future team leader, as well as bringing with them new skills to add to those of the team as a whole. If the selection process fails, one faulty cog can cause a ripple effect. Creating a culture that operates the leader-leader model requires competency throughout each level of the business. Without putting too fine a point on it, each and every team in your organisation needs to make a valued contribution in order to fulfil the overall purpose. Incompetence at any level simply derails the process. There is often also too much emphasis on being a team player. The problem here is that teams are also where the incompetent like to hide. Good leadership is about seeking out and developing highly-skilled individuals first and foremost; recognising them for both their own unique skills and performance and their contribution as a team member. Embedding these individuals into the team successfully is what good leaders do – it's all about alignment.

It is really important that you develop a coordinated recruitment strategy across your business. By this, I mean you should agree a *method* of selection. One that is consistent between departments and focuses on quality. The ultimate aim is to seek and obtain the best talent. This is not about the process of recruitment. It is about the selection strategy: one that can be clearly recognised by anyone inside and outside the business. Businesses need to be well orchestrated, operate with a natural rhythm and value the potential of every new member. As a leadership trait, this sits very high up the list of must-have skills. Of equal importance is how you then blend new recruits into your team. If you have been diligent in your selection process, the chances of seeing an early return on your investment is more likely. We are all familiar with the true cost of bringing new recruits through. Regardless of the level at which they join your organisation, there must be a clear and supported path to enable them to slot in. My experience tells me, and I have witnessed it far too often, that many managers fail their new recruits in the first few months by leaving them to their own devices. It tends to be a trait of the busy leader-follower manager or those leaders who are unable to effectively guide and coach.

Putting it into practice:

- Is your approach to recruitment a process or a strategy?
- Are you selecting high-quality talent at all levels?
- Are your team leaders good at recruiting, and do they look after new starters?
- Can you identify departmental patterns of retention rates for new starters?
- How could you invest your time better to improve the quality of selection?
- Consider the talent pool you already have that could be deployed elsewhere.

Chapter 5

Developing Your Team

As we discussed in Chapter 4, training and development is critical to staff retention and intimately connected to successful recruitment. For new hires, and for those who have been in the business for years, being nurtured and allowed to grow within the team will help them engage with their roles and perform at their best. It's also how to retain and attract new clients. If you expect your clients to pay for the very best, then you have to invest to provide that. They will ultimately recognise the true value of your team and will keep coming back for more. Let me illustrate with a personal story. I once went to visit a school with my eldest son, who was looking at various choices for his secondary education. During our tour, the principal stood up to address an audience of about 300 parents and their children. He made no apology for the slightly tired building that we were sitting in and drew our attention to the quality of his teaching staff and his passion about investing in the very best. He was a man of great experience, heading up one of the best schools in the county. That afternoon he clearly articulated that he knew the success of his school and our children's future was in the hands of his staff, and he wasn't going to compromise on that. He would simply paint the school another day.

When it comes to training and development, there are so many approaches open to you. The key is consistency. I acknowledge that in your day-to-day business, there are times when you just need to trade and get on with the job at hand. However, there are times when you must step back from operations and invest in developing and growing your business in order to move forward. The art of being a good leader, includes balancing the need to maintain today's performance with improving your chances for tomorrow. This is where the size of your direct team can grossly affect your ability to influence the development of others. It requires a regular investment of time and is certainly easier and more productive if your teams are of a manageable size. The same goes for all department heads and leaders throughout your organisation.

If your goal is to operate in a world of high alignment and high autonomy, you will need a robust personnel development strategy. Creating home-grown future leaders has so many benefits, as well as deepening a company's culture. The overriding aim is to breed a culture where alignment to a central purpose becomes second nature, allowing individuals and teams to travel in the right direction automatically. This will allow you the time to focus on your leadership development programme without the risk of veering off course. For real growth and success, you need to be constantly looking to share autonomy, encouraging competent individuals to intuitively respond to complex tasks and take the initiative with a can-do attitude. This is not to be confused with autonomy without true alignment. In the early part of our Fastnet campaign, it was clear that I had characters who were capable of making decisions and who in fact did exactly that, but often without any reference to a common goal. You are not looking to create decision-making silos.

It requires a strategy that clearly defines the boundaries and parameters of each individual's autonomy so a natural balance

Chapter 5: Developing Your Team

is struck. This allows each and every member of the business to express themselves by taking the lead and to freely operate within their defined area of responsibility. If we are good leaders ourselves, we will focus on removing the constraints to continuous personnel development in this way.

But can there be downsides to training and development. How should we handle these? To truly take a team on a development journey, you need to take a considerate approach to managing any change that could impact team members. It is too easy to assume that every individual wants to go on a development journey with you. Many are very happy with where they are and content within their role. Change or enforced learning can be quite daunting to some, and it might be the case that an individual requires a more subtle approach to development that can be delivered through guiding and coaching. This is not about mothering them, but taking a thoughtful approach to understanding any potential negative impact to their general wellbeing. See it through their eyes before you ask them to look at anything from your perspective. If, due to your company structure, you are personally unable to adopt this approach with the wider team, layer your organisation so that other leaders in the group can deliver support at this level. A team needs a leader who respects and understands their role and who makes considerate decisions based on this knowledge. In business we spend a lot of time working on the "why", "what", "where", "how" and "when". But it is the "who" within your organisation that make the real difference. They should be protected and nurtured for long-term success.

Consistent training and retraining are key if you want to develop tomorrow's home-grown, intuitive leaders. There is real value in offering accelerated learning to certain team members. For example, it may be beneficial to the business to reduce an individual's day-to-day workload in order for them to spend extra time developing their skillset. Potentially this route can provide a far better return on investment than having to recruit new staff with the appropriate skills. It may be the case that, in order to expedite the learning process, the individual also needs to invest some of their own time. This can be supported by the employer, such as funding evening classes. What is training? It can be a more formal plan to expand knowledge using courses and in-house training programmes, or it can simply be a matter of sharing stories and analogies in a controlled environment. Seek out the experts, both internally and externally, and listen to their hard-won experience. Share internal experiences of problems solved and failures encountered, and debate the lessons that can be learnt. Regularly creating these opportunities will allow individuals to build on their own understanding organically. Creating a learning culture has such value when it is delivered in a structured and recorded manner.

I must add that it is essential that your team are working as one, towards the same purpose and end goal, before you can embed a successful learning culture. In the development of the Fastnet team, it was only once we had become truly aligned that we were able to successfully take the team on a learning journey. In this more open and collaborative mindset, they soon recognised the value of the lessons shared and nuggets of insight from the experts. They successfully blended this new learning with their own experience and understanding, and we were all able to grow symbiotically as a group.

In sailing, a good proportion of the training you receive as a skipper is about avoiding danger. But it is virtually impossible to truly replicate real-life threats in a training environment. This can have an impact on your team's ability to respond in a real crisis. Inevitably, when you face an unknown force, you assimilate your approach by drawing on your experience of a lesser threat and work that up. Therefore, the stories of those that have found themselves in these scenarios before become invaluable tools. They will form part of the picture you will build in your mind to tackle your own unforeseen, and often unpractised, life or business challenges. To be a great skipper or leader, you need to seek out stories to fill the gaps in your experience.

This speaks to the importance of seeking out experts as mentors in training and development. However, there is sometimes a natural resistance to this approach. No doubt you will have seen that many avoid it, mainly due to the threat of being outshone or an unwillingness to accept alternative ideas. This is common in immature managers who are attempting to build their own authority. But they are simply missing opportunities to grow and develop. In order to navigate around this reluctance in your team, you need to ensure the content is of a high quality, with a clear purpose and is tailored to specific individuals. In fact, there often needs to be a thoughtful coaching plan when you're trying to embed business skills which are more of an art than a science. When you are delivering regular and prescriptive on-the-job training, such as operational techniques, compliance work, health and safety or administration requirements, it's a lot simpler. Team members understand that they are learning a generic set of guidelines or a method in order to complete basic tasks. There is little room for flair and creativity, and therefore individuals are often not as threatened by the prospect of learning new skills.

As leaders, this is where we need to focus our efforts. Our ability to effectively coach and guide our teams, inspiring true growth in individuals, is the real difference we can make to a business. Managing a team in a prescriptive way by focusing only on completing tasks harks back to the days of scientific management when employees were seen as productivity robots. As mentioned before, there is potentially still a place for this, as some tasks and businesses require this level of management and supervision. There are certain repetitive tasks carried out by individuals that only require simple direction. Factory lines, packing houses and deliveries are a few examples. However, in order to develop a business that benefits from the leader-leader model, we need to incorporate this ethos into the training strategy. One that offers employees the confidence to take control of their projects and lead their teams effectively, which then frees up leaders from running the business day to day. We need to train them to be independent and creative thinkers who can make their own decisions in pursuit of a shared goal.

At this level, training needs to provide value both to the participant and to the business. The employee needs to recognise the value to them beyond that which is immediately gained by the business. If they can see the benefits to their overall personal development, they are more likely to respond to training. As I said earlier, it's important to recruit the strongest individuals as a priority. We can then work on how to blend them into a functional group with a common purpose. As leaders, we need to be able to motivate them towards this goal. But what do we need to be able to do this? I am a firm believer in the idea that if you truly understand your team members as individuals, then you can successfully tailor high-quality training for them to this end. Understanding your team members' unique and preferred way of operating is critical to the success of your organisation. Ignore it at your peril. If you are a seasoned developer of people, then you will intuitively know who goes where and how best to blend individuals to make a rounded team. If not, then you can rely on sharing your personal traits and behaviours as a team to enrich your understanding. Many years ago, I was introduced to one of the better personality analysis tools which was used to great effect. Myers Briggs enables us to see where people's strengths and weaknesses lie and why they act or react in certain ways. It's not about overanalysing with full-on psychometric testing; they aren't training to become fighter pilots or astronauts. However, some insight into your key players' tendencies can go a long way to avoiding conflict, creating better cohesion and finding the right position and path for each individual to shine.

Investing in training and development is a business priority if you want to successfully and sustainably grow.

Putting it into practice:

- Take time out to assess the success and failure you've had in training new recruits.
- How current is your leadership training programme?
- How do you monitor training and retraining across the business?
- Is the training offered clearly tailored to the individual?
- Consider what type of training would be required to create a 10% improvement in the output of your team.
- Do you understand the behavioural traits of your team members, and do your plans take into account this understanding?

The Story of the Fastnet Race, Part 4: *The Race*

As we got closer to the start date, I could sense a calmness and confidence within the team. There was a better understanding of each other's abilities and the yacht itself. We had a rhythm that was sound, and now it was just a case of heading off to that famous start line. I was going to lead the team into an environment that was new to us all.

The day before the start of the race, the senior navigator and myself took a ferry trip over to the Isle of Wight. We were to attend the official weather forecast briefing, where representatives from each team get an insight into the predictions for the coming days. This is delivered by one of the country's leading sailing meteorologists, and it's a big moment for the teams. Weather is a huge factor in your planning and is both friend and foe to the sailor. This was probably the biggest "what if" within our planning strategy and would require constant tracking and evaluation if we wanted to harness its value. Once on board, predicting the weather is certainly an art and, even though forecasts are produced by highly-sophisticated computer software, interpretation is often in the hands of the skipper. During the official briefing they predicted relatively calm weather for the period, with mainly light winds. This particular region has a reputation for being a little unpredictable and things can get quite interesting, so we remained open-minded. However, it seemed that our biggest challenge could in fact be keeping the yacht going forwards against some of the strong tides.

In a sailing race of this type, you cannot use your engine at any time to gain an advantage, or to even hold your position in a strong tide. If becalmed at any time, dropping your anchor is often the only option to avoid going backwards, and it's only available to you if the water is shallow enough to allow it. This news of calm winds and strong tides had put quite a slant on our campaign, and I'm sure it was a concern for lots of other teams too. Right up until the starting cannon, many of the professional teams were continuously updating their weather models. They were also taking some quite drastic measures in order to reduce weight on their yachts. Quite simply, your crew and kit become the ballast on a sailing yacht, and this can be added to or taken away depending on the prevailing weather conditions. If there is little wind for you to utilise, you need a light boat to reduce drag; if there are strong winds, then you have more room for manoeuvre. For many teams with the goal of winning their class honours or being first across the line, their only choice was to reduce their crew numbers. This certainly wasn't an option for us. I think my leadership of an amateur racing team may have ended at that point with a mutiny. Our aims and agenda were quite different from those professional teams. Although bigger winds would have suited our team dynamics, our purpose and ambitions remained sound. As a token nod to our predicament, I asked each team member to re-evaluate all items that they were bringing on board and reduce them to a minimum level that was still safe. This had already been requested as part of the general good seamanship approach, but we felt it was worth a second round of trimming. However, many of us were still amused to see what comfort items people had tucked into their kit bag. One crew member had slightly overprepared for the end of race celebrations and had packed his Saturday night grooming kit, including his heavyweight electric shaver.

Whilst we were at the weather briefing and completing the final administrative tasks ashore, the remaining crew were completing the final preparations to the yacht. All victuals and kit had been strategically packed on board. During my absence, the watch leaders had made an executive decision between them that, on the completion of all tasks, they would retire to the local marina bar to toast their achievements so far. It was only after the race had started the next day, and during our first major sail change, that I noticed a level of lethargy amongst the team. Later they would all share with me the extent of that earlier toast ashore. The visit to the marina bar certainly didn't feature in my plan or in the back brief given by my watch leaders. Fittingly, they botched the first sail drop, but it was heartening to witness them all making it good and looking after one another as a unit. This was a classic example to me of allowing your leaders the space to interpret your intentions. My instruction to them was to ensure the boat was ready to go 12 hours before the start. To be fair, that was immaculately achieved by each and every one of them. They were forgiven for their slow start, and I learnt to never tell your crew that it will be a calm and easy first 24 hours.

Over the next four days at sea, the weather we experienced was more or less according to the earlier predictions. This allowed the team to settle easily into their watch systems. As it happened, two thirds of the overall distance we sailed was mainly towards the wind. That meant that, on the whole, we were able to maintain a relatively good pace, if not always in the perfect direction. This type of sailing race requires you to continuously pay attention to the numbers. This was a long-distance race, and for the less experienced crew it can be easy to slip into cruising mode. However, unless you are continuously keeping up to date with the natural changes around you and how they're impacting your speed or direction, it's very easy to lose a few valuable hours every day. We needed to ensure that the yacht was performing at its optimum pace for the given wind strength, direction and sea state. It was now a simple case of monitoring and recording how well we were doing in comparison to our plan. It was also important to make sure there was enough going on to keep the team focused during their watch period. It was easy to lose concentration after several hours of staring at an unchanging sea with little to do in terms of adjusting sails or making a significant course alteration. It was important that the team remained engaged so we didn't miss an opportunity, but this needed to be balanced with avoiding the temptation to tweak the rig out of boredom. These conditions also meant that getting the right amount of sleep was achievable, which helped the team remain motivated and in good spirits.

During the race, my main focus was ensuring we retained the discipline to continuously operate at our best. It wasn't unusual to be sailing in open water without another competitor in sight. We had to assume that those we were competing against were also potentially being challenged by the calmer conditions and remember that places could be won and lost each hour if we took our eyes off the ball. As leader I had to ensure the team understood the bigger picture. The reporting systems we had put in place gave each and every crew member the opportunity to remain fully engaged with our overall progress. In fact, and often due to the lack of other tasks available for the team, I made it my goal to share as much information as possible in terms of understanding the numbers. It was also the perfect opportunity for the team to widen their understanding and learn more about the tactical and strategic considerations that both myself and the navigator were dealing with. Alongside this, and during these quieter moments, the watch leaders and their teams ensured the equipment on board remained at its best. In fact, they found a couple of issues that could have caught us out later in the passage. As skipper and navigator, you spend a lot of time re-evaluating your strategy. As each opportunity presented itself, small deviations were made to take advantage of a changing picture. They could be as simple as altering course to take advantage of a changing tide or reconfiguring the sail to benefit from either a reduction or increase in wind. We carried a total of eight sails on board, and most of the time we sailed with a combination of two. So, quite a choice. There were times when suggestions were made for changes but, tempting as it was to improve our progress in that moment, many of these proposals failed to fully consider the overall goal. In lighter wind conditions it can be tempting to chase a favourable tide too far, but you then pay a price later in terms of your position relative to the wind as it fills back in. It certainly isn't a science; it's more the art of constantly juggling the pros and cons. Having the ability to detach yourself from the moment became key to each leader when making strategic decisions.

To further aid our understanding regarding the numbers, on board we had a satellite phone. Although you were not allowed to rely on a shore-based team to help with your campaign, it did allow us to touch base with our shore contact. Many of our families and friends were tracking us on their computer screens to see our progress. This information wasn't available to us from the equipment on board, and it certainly helped us to understand how we were doing compared to others. Throughout the race we had a high-level progress report and, in fact, with 24 hours to go, we noticed the yacht of a friend only about eight miles ahead of us. As a final challenge, and to maintain our focus in these closing stages, we decided to pursue a mini-goal of catching this other competitor. This proved to be very motivational to the team, as the yacht in question was similar to our own but carrying less crew. The wind had begun to fill in nicely, and this final leg saw the wind behind us. For those of you with a bit of sailing knowledge, we were now able to fly our large spinnaker sail.

This mini-challenge, although motivational, was risky. There was a danger we might be encouraged to repeat the errors of the vessel in front. As it is in business, you can be so focused on the battle in front of you, and on picking off your main competitor, that you fail to realise the rest of the fleet have altered course and found a new and better route. In failing to concentrate on your own journey, you lose sight of your core purpose and the bigger picture. However, although determined to stay focused on beating the course, we set our targets on catching this yacht and had satisfied ourselves that the benefits outweighed the potential losses. Sailing a traditional monohulled vessel is a relatively slow affair, and it would be some time before we would actually gain clear sight of this yacht by the naked eye. Regardless, the crew became healthily obsessed with spotting and catching our target. After about 10 hours of chipping away, we could clearly make out the other boat some two miles ahead of us. We headed inshore to take advantage of the next turn of the tide. We continued to push hard and to close the gap further, but it took some time. With about four hours to go, and now in complete darkness, we certainly had a mini-race on our hands. It had become clear that this yacht had the same idea as us, and you could sense they were pulling out all the stops to maintain their now small lead. The breeze had freshened, and we were on the limit of continuing to carry our large spinnaker sail. Plus, the sea state was now building.

There is a point (due to each yacht's unique design) at which the vessel becomes overpowered and difficult to handle. You have to balance the increase in speed against how the yacht is handling. Push too far and you run the risk of being out of control. Although being near the edge all the time, the wind remained at a steady level. We were therefore happy to proceed as we were and agreed not to change the sail configuration.

Our run into the finish line was going to be highly energetic and a lot of fun. My concern was that we would lose our concentration in the heat of the moment and risk injury or even potentially lose a crew member overboard. So, for the first time in the race, I called for complete silence on the boat and asked that, for the final hour, we stayed fully focused on our safety. It was becoming clear that we were going to be entering the final run into the finishing line with seven or eight other yachts, in complete darkness, all wishing to complete this iconic race ahead of each other.

After we had established some clear boundaries on board our yacht, I was now happy to carry on pushing as hard as we could. We were now travelling quicker than at any other time in the race, with just 45 minutes left. It was now impossible to track what that other yacht was up to, but that ceased to be our focus at the end. All concentration and communication were given over to managing this final moment, to guarantee we would complete it in one piece. We stormed through the finish line, with three other boats very close to us.

Even though we'd finished the race, we still had to negotiate getting the sails down and starting our engine, all whilst avoiding other yachts, the harbour wall and with one eye on the fresh breeze and bouncy sea. Holding back the natural elation and celebration within the team for just a few minutes was key to making sure we didn't fall at the last hurdle. Within a few minutes, the team had efficiently started the engine and dropped the sails. We then allowed ourselves a moment of celebration, before motoring into our reserved mooring for the night. As we got nearer to the berth, we could see on the pontoon our friend and crew member who had had to withdraw from the team, waiting to welcome us home with cold bottles of bubbly.

Even though it was now 2am, we were full of adrenaline and the joy of completing such an iconic race, so we took ourselves ashore and toured a number of bars. As we got off the boat, I did feel the urge to disappear for a moment on my own for the first time for five days. I reflected briefly on what we had achieved, and I was choked. The last 24 hours had been awe-inspiring, not only because of our accomplishment but also because of what the team members had said to me as we finished.

For the record, we finished in 202nd place. After 135 hours of racing, we were beaten by 45 seconds by the boat we targeted on the last day. And yes, I did lay awake for a month thinking about where we could have come with laminated sails. Five percent quicker and we would have finished in 125th place overall.

Chapter 6

Embracing Failure as a Tool

Before we delve deeper into what we have discussed so far and how it may shape our approach to strategic planning within business, I want to share with you my take on failure. The *Oxford English Dictionary* defines it as: "Lack of success, non-success, non-fulfilment, defeat, frustration, collapse." It is also defined within the same dictionary as "the neglect or omission of expected or required action, or the state or condition of not meeting a desirable or intended objective."

Reading emotive words like 'defeat' or 'collapse', you can see why many people act in a style of failure avoidance. By entertaining the idea of failure, you seem to be welcoming oblivion into your home. Strict failure avoidance has its place, of course, when the stakes are very high. For example, the racing driver or climber who pushes the boundaries of their sport so far to the edge that it actually claims their lives. The same goes for those businesses whose employees are exposed to physical danger simply because of the job they do, such as those working on construction sites. It is the director's responsibility to avoid that type of failure at all costs. But blanket failure avoidance is also incredibly damaging as it stymies the creativity needed for growth and development; the willingness to fail and our resilience in the face of failure is, in fact, absolutely critical to our progress.

On that basis, I don't recommend failure avoidance but a strategic plan to deal with risk. It seems to me that one of two main components are often present when failure occurs: lack of experience and talent or lack of discipline. A good strategy has to consider the obvious risks as well as factor in the unknowns; it's all about calculating and controlling potential problems rather than circumventing them altogether. This is because, to be very successful, you need to venture as far as you dare in the pursuit of greater understanding and knowledge. Fortune favours the brave. Remember Winston Churchill's famous quote: *"Success is not final and failure is not fatal. It is the courage to continue that counts."*

For failure avoiders, the safest route is to do nothing; with no attempt, there can be no failure. Planning to fail would be foolish, of course. However, it's also foolish to think that sustained success occurs before a breakthrough. Several failures are often necessary in order to reach your intended goal; those of us that are striving for perfection or looking to widen our experience understand and accept failure as a progressive step; it forms part of our momentum. However, as my mother would remind me in my youth, a learning curve is fine as long as it doesn't become a circle, returning you to the very beginning. Many years on, that still rings loud and clear in my head.

When we put the Fastnet campaign together, we were constrained by our lack of available training time. As a new team, simulating the likely race conditions was impossible in the few weekends we had. We were thus heavily reliant on the previous experience of team members. However, we shared stories of previous lessons learnt and also went outside the team to gain the insight of experts who had valuable stories to tell. Understanding how and why others had failed and, most importantly, what had been learnt, certainly helped to structure our own thoughts and

Chapter 6: Embracing Failure as a Tool

plans. In this way we could analyse the most likely risks we would encounter and consider how to manage them. Our journey, by its very nature, would never be risk-free. Our strategy was to embrace and learn from those risks and prevent them from undermining the whole campaign.

I was once listening to a seasoned athlete being interviewed after he had just won his first ever Olympic gold medal. He eloquently described his world of continuous development and training. He paid what must have seemed at that time in his young life a huge price of having to choose between his childhood friendships (that were potentially taking him in the wrong direction) and his desire to compete in sport. Ultimately, he chose to dedicate his youth and early adulthood to competitive sport. Often dogged by injury and having to put up with regular defeat, he had to dig deep and persevere whilst being acutely aware that anything less than first place is often perceived as failure. Ultimately, however, failures that he had grown used to, and that he was able to learn from and harness gave him the focus and energy that would see him reach the top of his sport. What was clear in the interview was that he had to draw on a great deal of self-discipline to carry on. This is the ultimate test of character in so many young sportsmen and sportswomen. When you compare it to other walks of life, it is truly remarkable. For many, they see failure as the end as opposed to a progressive step. The value of their coaching team is never underestimated, as it is those coaches that tell the stories of failure and success that will help them to persevere.

A fear of failure is so evident in many people within the workplace. You can see it in their decision-making, you can feel it in their plans and you can hear it in the language they use. Individuals that possess this trait will never really give a clear instruction and often delay or avoid making a decision, appearing non-committal. It can be quite entertaining to sit back and listen to these individuals. You will notice that, when talking, they avoid any reference to personal accountability. They use phrases like "we can have a look at that", "I'll have a go – but...", "I can't promise anything" and "we'll have to see how it goes". Just imagine stepping onto a plane and the captain seeming vague in his intentions during his announcement – not exactly a confidence builder for the passengers. These individuals like operating in teams. If there is potential for failure, they prefer it to be as a group. It often goes far beyond being risk averse; it is often true discomfort with being held accountable for failure. These same people are often very quick to criticise others and, in fact, gain some sort of satisfaction out of watching others fail. These individuals lack the self-confidence and the discipline required to take action themselves, yet they find it easy and, sadly, sometimes rewarding to disrupt the path that others are seeking to take. Good leaders know how to recognise these patterns of behaviour and will structure their teams so that it has no impact. When operating in a silo culture, as in box four of the alignment and autonomy framework, you run a high risk of this unhealthy individual personality trait becoming a team trait. If a leader struggles with accountability and passes the buck for their failings, you often end up with a team that is a reflection of that leader. Each and every team member will avoid accountability and, in some cases, they will sweep failure under the carpet to avoid exposure. In these cases, project reviews become a blame game between departments as opposed to a rich resource of learning for the wider business. You have to recognise that these individuals may have developed this trait due to being punished or chastised in the past for failure. So, some employees display these characteristics not by choice but in order to avoid the wrath of their inconsiderate boss.

Chapter 6: Embracing Failure as a Tool

Failure is an inevitable and quite necessary component of our existence. Limit it where you can and expose it where needed to provide direction, but make sure that you embrace it, savour it and learn from it. Remember that it is a by-product of dedication and hard work that ultimately creates new understanding; it is a tool of progress. Therefore, as a good leader, it is not a case of just forgiving yourself or others, as you would a child who says sorry. You need to know the "why" if it is to be of any value to anyone, including those that failed.

Putting it into practice:

- Think about how you have positively dealt with your own failures in the past and what lessons you can draw from this strategy.
- How do you generally respond to failure in others?
- Does your business capture, correct and control consistent failures?
- Consider what training you have in place to allow others to learn from mistakes.

The Story of a Novice Skipper

We are now at the end of our story of the Fastnet race, but let me tell you another tale recounted to me by a sailing student of mine. In embarking on a new challenge, a difficult and chaotic baptism of fire, he was able to learn many lessons. As I've said before, this only highlights the importance of sharing stories and drawing from others' experience and your own failures. It also speaks to some of the key insights we've touched on throughout the book around the importance of team composition as well as good communication, alignment and autonomy.

This mature student was at the very beginning of his journey to become an offshore skipper. He had previously and successfully managed a number of small, daylight-hour passages, all of which had been carried out with an experienced mentor on board. On this particular occasion, he wanted to push himself further and make his first skippered passage across the English Channel to France. He had chartered a 40-foot sailing yacht, enrolled a couple of his friends as novice crew and had enlisted the support of an old associate who was a very experienced yachtsman. The experienced yachtsman had agreed to accompany the crew to not only satisfy the charter company's criteria for experience on board, but to act as a relatively hands-off mentor, in order for the up-and-coming skipper to test himself. The proposed passage was 70 miles, with an anticipated journey time of around 12 hours.

SHIPSHAPE

They were due to pick up the yacht at 2pm on the Friday and return it back at 9am on the Monday. The skipper had diligently laid out his detailed passage plan the night before, and they were all on board ready to go at about 3pm. The weather had been rather windy over the previous few days. In fact, when they arrived at the boat, the wind was still quite strong, so they opted to delay setting off until later that evening. The forecast was predicting calmer conditions to follow, and the weather window for the weekend was improving.

As time passed an atmosphere of impatience began to brew. They were keen to get on with the plan and, although the wind was still relatively strong, the first couple of hours of the passage were in the lee of an island that would protect them from the worst of the blow, with a forecast stating that it was due to reduce imminently. They made the decision to set sail; lines were slipped at around 10pm, and away they went. The first couple of hours were relatively busy whilst they safely navigated themselves out of the busy harbour and prepared to meet their first key waypoint. As they cleared the island, it soon became apparent that the sea state was still quite lively, with the previous days' gale leaving its mark. Although the wind was reducing, they still had at least 15 - 20 knots of breeze and, together with a lumpy sea, it was apparent that it was going to be an interesting few hours. They pushed on, and over the next couple of hours the relatively novice crew were beginning to feel the effects of the sea, made slightly worse by being in complete darkness and in an unfamiliar setting. The plan had originally assumed that, by midnight, two people would be on watch, whilst the other two got some rest. Unfortunately, in quite a short period of time, the crew, including the budding skipper, had all become rather tired, and they had to turn to the experienced yachtsman for some guidance as they all needed to rest. The old

The Story of a Novice Skipper

hand suggested reducing the sail area to slow the boat down, which effectively reduced the impact of the lumpy sea. He also suggested altering course slightly in order to reduce the amount of trimming required (adjusting of sails), which in turn allowed the novice crew member who was steering a far easier task. He then suggested that the skipper and one of the crew got their heads down for an hour or so whilst he covered for them. After being at sea for a total of six hours, the mentor and active crew member needed some shut eye of their own, so they swapped over with the other two. Thankfully, this small amount of rest had had the desired effect, and the skipper was now clearly back in control of the plan. Although the sea state hadn't yet abated, they were now set up to better manage the task ahead. Due to the actions that the mentor had suggested, the original plan that the skipper had prepared had somewhat changed. His role was now to manage the boat and, in order to arrive at the chosen destination, he needed to work up a revised strategy. What was originally forecasted to be a 12-hour passage was now looking something nearer to a 16-hour one. Ahead of them, they still had busy shipping lanes to navigate, and unfortunately, the mentor, who suffered from diabetes, was experiencing a mild illness that had made him slightly delirious. Plus, to add to the new skipper's problems, the crew member who had been off watch had woken feeling rather seasick and had taken himself off into a quiet corner of the cabin.

Imagine this for a moment: you are embarking on a pretty challenging task; it's pitch black other than the dim lights in the distance of huge vessels in the shipping lanes you are soon to be crossing; and your safety net of a mentor who was holding things together has just been incapacitated. It would be hard to deal with this situation under normal circumstances, let alone that you, the only crew member left standing, have only had 90 minutes' sleep. Remember they are at sea; it is certainly not comfortable, and the wind is still blowing quite strong. Everybody is a little tired or not very well, and right now there is a general feeling of clutching at straws. That said, the now somewhat challenged skipper did not panic and decided to again seek the guidance of his mentor regarding the next alteration of course. He was well prepared, having produced lots of numbers and options to support his various strategies of getting back on track. He recognised that they were in no immediate danger, as he had experienced crossing the shipping lanes as a crew member a number of times before. The major difference was that this time it was he who was making the final decisions. After presenting the mentor with the various options, they agreed to alter course slightly away from the shipping lanes and their destination, in order to allow things to calm down a bit and wait for sunrise. They would then put themselves back on track when things were a little clearer and calmer. As it happens, they were so far behind their original plan that, in fact, altering course away from their port would be offset later by a favourable tide.

The passage had already been quite a challenge, but what happened next is really quite astonishing. Unfortunately, in the slightly chaotic and fragile set-up that they had found themselves in, a miscommunication between them continued to add to their troubles. The skipper, who had spent much time at the chart table working all this out, called up to the crew member on the helm and asked him to alter course to 205 degrees. Due to the conditions, the helm misheard and repeated 295 degrees. Then, distracted by writing up his log, the skipper loudly replied, "Yes, as I said, 295 degrees". Even though the novice crew member had enough understanding to realise that this was actually tacking the boat through the wind, he felt that the skipper must know what he was doing and simply altered course and adjusted the sails to suit.

The skipper was oblivious to the alteration of course and continued to diligently write up his notes. It wasn't until an hour later, when making up the log, that the skipper realised the error and, again, altered course. They had extended their journey even more and, in fact, were heading in completely the wrong direction.

It wasn't long before the sun came up, and the sea was finally calming down. The wind had dropped considerably, and both the mentor and other crew member were now feeling much better and able to give the others a well-earned break. They did eventually arrive at their chosen port. However, it was not for lunch as planned, but for a sumptuous evening meal, full of the stories of the night before. So, what can we learn from this story? This simple, true account of a passage being made by a trainee skipper is full of valuable lessons for others to learn from. You may well say that hindsight is a wonderful thing and we could never guess that this particular combination of events would occur. And, indeed, the belief that the outcome of events is easy to predict (termed hindsight bias) is often used in business to apportion blame. However, this story of failure (and success) is still a rich source of information to be shared and debated with those that seek to learn and widen their own understanding. If you are a leader who makes critical decisions, seeking to understand where others went wrong so as to highlight what *not* to do often has as much value as trying to establish the right course of action.

However, if you want these stories to truly alter and add to the thinking of others, they have to be delivered in a controlled and measured way. In a classroom environment, I have used this simple account of a weekend passage many times with new skippers. Without going into the really technical aspects of the discussion, listed below is a brief example of some of the basic questions and suggestions that came from the team in a training session. This approach may help you to understand how to tackle the learning process when it comes to analysing stories of failure.

Analytical questions:

- Why did they leave at 10pm? What was the urgency to get underway?
- Was the crew composition capable of making a passage of this length in the forecasted conditions?
- With regards to sea state, did the skipper have enough understanding of how this particular stretch of water would be affected by the direction and strength of the wind, together with the influence of the tide?
- Should they have turned back at any time? Do you think the comfort of having an experienced yachtsman on board as a mentor influenced the skipper's judgement in this regard?
- Was it wise to plan to spend so much of the passage at night? Had the plan been to spend as much of the weekend as possible ashore in France, and had that influenced the skipper's judgement?
- What had the skipper built into his plan regarding alternative destinations?
- Had the skipper considered what might happen if the mentor became incapacitated?
- How much time during the passage had the skipper spent with his head buried in the chart table?
- Was this new skipper biased towards the art of navigation, and did he have less experience of good seamanship?

Suggestions for answers:

- The weather forecast supported a delayed departure. Regardless of the forecast, the local conditions continued to demonstrate that the weather remained uncertain. As they were ready to go at 3pm, they could have set off on a three- or four-hour familiarisation sail in the safety of the local protected waters. This would have given the whole team an opportunity to get a feel for and understanding of the yacht as well as working as a team. This has the added advantage of the yacht being back alongside a pontoon before 7pm, with a crew that would have been looking forward to a meal and a good period of sleep before embarking on the main passage the next day.
- Putting the mentor to one side, this crew was certainly novice in terms of making a busy channel crossing at night and in adverse weather conditions. They had put pressure on themselves to continue, although there was a clear option to abort after three hours. The mentor offered the skipper a safety net. However, if the intention of the passage was to test the skipper's judgement and ability without relying on the mentor, the crew members were certainly lacking experience for such a passage with a novice leader.
- The skipper had originally planned to slip at 3pm (assuming this suited his initial navigation plan) and therefore was planning to arrive in a foreign port in the middle of the night. Regardless of the challenge of the weather, it may have been better to have planned the majority of the night hours in waters that he was familiar with. In this way he'd

be crossing the shipping lanes and scheduling the arrival within a large daylight window. Slipping at, say, 4am instead, after all the crew had been nourished and had slept for a period, would have contributed towards a more balanced passage.
- Having a back-up passage plan, to an altogether different destination that suited the weather conditions, would have reduced the pressure to proceed as originally planned.
- The skipper had diligently planned the passage well in advance, but less consideration had been given to crew competency and what he might do if something happened to the mentor. The passage plan he created needed to genuinely consider the depth and breadth of his experience and knowledge. Although you have to push the boundaries in order to improve and grow, you can leap too far. The skipper had the intelligence to enlist the support of a mentor but, when choosing to slip at 10pm that night, he had already committed to a passage well beyond his and the crew's abilities. He could have adopted a number of other strategies in order to mitigate some of the risks that were being taken. His almost immediate reliance on the mentor clearly demonstrated that he had bitten off too much.

When the skipper shared this story with me, he said that he had learnt so much from the experience. He was acutely aware that the passage could have easily turned into something quite serious if the mentor had been completely incapacitated. It helped him realise that his real passion was as a navigator and that this had also been his downfall in this instance. The reality was that he had a desire to challenge his abilities by independently navigating to France, on a passage that was out of sight of land. I got to know this gentleman well as he sailed with me a number of times. He was a great mathematician, but he wasn't a skipper who could simultaneously balance the art of passage planning with that of leading a small team.

So, what can we learn here when it comes to training and development? There is so much to be gained from seeking out training modules that accelerate learning; training that identifies hidden strengths early, enhancing the participants' understanding in a short period of time. In most businesses, it is difficult to deliver in-house training of this type. Consider taking your team into a different environment, away from their normal surroundings. Look for environments that create a context in which communication, trust, alignment, autonomy and team composition management can all be tested and honed in a relatively short period of time. When I have taken business leaders and their teams out on the water for two or three days, they are always surprised by how this different environment, together with a number of well-structured tasks, stimulates communication and quickly encourages the team to work as one. Most teams in a foreign environment, when facing a new task, will naturally seek out the strengths in individual team members. They soon recognise that if they combine these strengths, they are more likely to succeed as a unit. Of course, it's a challenge and can be delivered at various levels. However, in my experience, these types of professionally-delivered, outward-bound courses geared towards team structure can really offer insight and a better understanding of the value of a leadership framework. These learnings can be easily consolidated, if followed up and reinforced through coaching in the workplace.

Chapter 7

The Skipper as Strategic Planner

Before we look into the art of strategic planning in business, I want to take you back to sea for a moment to consider the skipper's role in terms of navigating. Every good yacht skipper has a deep understanding of the art of navigation, and thus of strategic planning. Firstly, their ability to travel is subject to their grasp of how to successfully shape and lay down a passage plan. Secondly, it is about their ability to make adjustments to the plan once momentum has started.

Most inexperienced skippers have paid the price for putting together a rushed or incomplete plan. For some this has proved catastrophic, and for others it meant that a journey was never completed. As a solo sailor, planning errors are felt by you alone, whereas the skipper who takes a crew with them has to deal with the wider impact on the team; much like a business leader's strategic errors will be felt like ripples by his direct reports and throughout the organisation.

During the early training phase of a skipper's life, the art of passage planning is developed in bite-sized chunks. These early practice sessions are often facilitated by an instructor on board. As with the armed services and in the world of sport, the skippers learning journey is one of repetition. To be very good, the theory behind the subject needs to be deeply understood, followed by their ability to apply this in a practical situation. Add to this the dimension of taking a team with you on this journey, and you now have what I believe to be the ultimate test of a team leader.

It is imperative that the skipper sets aside quality time to consider and shape the passage plan. In a clear and structured manner, decisions need to be made with regards to where, when and how the plan is likely to be executed. Consideration will be given to the resources available, and the ability and competency level of the crew will play a fundamental role in the overall strategy. A simple short passage, in familiar waters and made during daylight hours, requires far less detail compared to a complex passage into foreign waters made over a number of days or weeks. As the leader, you recognise that the competency level of the team will ultimately set the pace and direction you choose. The more complex the plan, the more reliance on those around you.

The uniqueness of operating 24 hours a day in a yacht at sea, combined with a changing and often tumultuous environment, creates a heightened level of focus. However, for the experienced skipper, this is as true when in the calmness of the harbour or when ashore and planning the passage as it is when at sea managing the yacht each day – they must retain a clear mind at all times. During the planning phase, the skipper is aware that the moment the yacht slips its moorings and heads out into the open sea, the plan becomes fluid and is subject to unknowns. Thus it not only reflects the intended route and strategy, but it has to consider alternative options in order to maintain momentum. Within the plan, there needs to be a healthy level of 'what ifs', and the more experienced the leader, the less this is likely to paralyse the planning process. Crucially, the plan needs a clear intent (ultimate goal), with defined gateways (objective milestones that demonstrate progress) and should be constructed with a deep level of integrity (considering the reality of its potential), all of which can be clearly measured and monitored during the passage, by both the skipper and the team responsible for its execution.

Once at sea, the skipper assesses, adapts and works with any challenges in order to maintain direction, altering course where needed to achieve the ultimate destination. They are tuned into seeing things before they happen and taking action to avoid critical failure. For example, when the skipper observes that the weather is likely to change for the worse, they set about preparing for that in advance. You learn the hard way if you wait for it to be upon you before taking action. Similarly, the leader watching the marketplace around them will try to predict trends before they impact the business. During the passage, there are times when decision making is required at speed. In these instances, the decision-making process changes and the leader's experience and ability to recognise patterns (intuition) becomes the preferred tool. Hindsight may prove that there were better options, but when something is time-critical, it is about how to make decisions based on what we can currently see. A slower process of weighing up all the options isn't always the best way forwards and can dilute the value of expertise. There are times when the last thing you need is to overanalyse and ultimately, as skipper, you will make a decision based on what option will work in the moment. Being able to stand by the decisions you make in these situations is what we do as leaders. However, it's important to acknowledge that we can only choose our intuition when we have developed enough experience to understand the potential consequences. Often, we are driven into making two or three quick decisions in a row in order to realign our path with our expectations. That style of operation is all quite normal for an expert, who is constrained by time and doesn't have the option to sit down and consider every possible alternative.

A clear indication of an expert navigator's thinking on board any vessel run by a professional team is the quality of the ship's log. It records and monitors the key components of every passage. It enables the skipper to continually update progress against the plan, helping to structure the thinking required to adapt and adjust the approach in order to arrive at the chosen destination. In this way, we can see how recording, reassessing and adjusting a plan is essential to good strategic thinking and, ultimately, to results. Great skippers are always working ahead of the boat. They anticipate the next move and expect the unexpected. What can this tell us about what it takes to become an expert business leader?

Putting it into practice:

- Do you set aside quality time to lay down your strategic business plan?
- Do you get your plan peer reviewed?
- Do you evaluate your team and consider how that analysis may shape the plan?
- Do you consider the 'what ifs' within your plan?
- How do you monitor and record progress against your plan?

Chapter 8
The Value of Strategic Planning

I have met many business managers who I would describe as journey seekers. They have developed and often mastered an approach to leading that 'has no final destination'. This type of leader states that the journey itself offers a rich source of learning with less boundaries and restrictions for team members. In reality, what I have witnessed with this "for the journey's sake" approach is a leader that has an unclear agenda and suffers from a continually altering course, all the time hiding behind the premise of "learning". They ultimately attract and recruit passengers who want to follow them on this journey, leading to similarly directionless teams that are focused on the moment and their own development as opposed to a goal which will enrich the business. When you investigate this approach further, businesses led and managed by this type of leader struggle to hold on to talented personnel and exist purely in the leader-follower model. They are to be avoided as leaders, as their lack of direction and clear decision-making creates trust issues with key players. Their teams become subservient to the journey manager and not the company as a whole. If you want real success, you need leaders who are happy to commit to an end goal. Those that have the courage to set out a plan that clearly maps out a route. Similarly, at sea, there are those that are happy to set sail and let wind and tide dictate the destination. This is a very romantic approach and extremely rewarding for those that have the time. In today's business world, that approach works only for the very few who are lucky enough to get swept onto rewarding shores. Good leaders know how to set a course and are willing to work against both wind and tide in order to progress, get ahead of the competition and ultimately sail towards new and profitable horizons. They know the value of strategic planning.

So, now we have the right leader – an expert navigator – how do we develop that strategic plan? Often businesses make some headway towards planning and strategy, but they don't achieve it in a holistic way. Most well-run businesses have a clear vision and a set of company values that form part of their alignment strategy with both their clients and employees. Indeed, when it comes to the various departments, they tend to use planning tools in the form of financial planning spreadsheets and project workflows. However, in terms of day-to-day trading, they tend to operate on a "business as usual" basis, which can be relatively reactive. In my experience, this is certainly more common in companies that have been established for some time. This chapter's focus is therefore about more formal and holistic strategic planning: plans that help to support a growth strategy and the management of complex initiatives.

Putting a new strategic plan together requires a dedicated commitment of time and resource. With many business plans failing to deliver on their promises at an early stage, it is key that you develop a systematic and disciplined approach to this task.

There are certain rules of thumb in regard to growth that are useful to consider when outlining your strategic plan. Most well-founded businesses experience early growth as they enter the market for the first time, and this won't necessarily continue after the honeymoon period. If they grow and expand their offering, momentum is often maintained for a period, but this isn't necessarily sustainable. There might be many reasons for a reduction in performance over time, such as a lack of particular skills within the organisation, the leader's reluctance to take a risk, or simply saturation of the market sector in which you are trading. Many businesses are launched based on offering either a completely new product or service that aligns with emerging trends or a better or more competitive solution aimed at an established market. Consider the airline industry. No doubt you can recall when new companies such as Ryanair entered the market simply to disrupt the status quo, catching out a number of established behemoths who were sitting on their laurels and failing to offer better value for money to customers. Some of the casualties in this scenario were previously perceived as successful as they had attracted a good share of the market place. Yet they ultimately failed to continually refresh their offering in order to stay ahead of the curve. Therefore, for a number of reasons, many businesses reach various trading limits from time to time; the ceiling of their current model has been reached, and it is at this time that many search for different ways to attract new income streams. Living in the world of organic growth (as opposed to strategic growth) is great; all the time it is in an upward trend and ahead of the rate of inflation without any high-level thinking required. However, it shouldn't be relied upon in the long term. As discussed above, this approach has a high level of risk and can expose the business to competitors who are proactively seeking more market share. Is your business simply following a positive market trend organically, or are you actively developing strategies that allow you to diversify and innovate competitively? You should ask yourself this question: would you invest your life savings in a business that relies only on organic growth?

SHIPSHAPE

The reality is, if you want to maintain a high level of control, you need a robust growth strategy; one that offers you the opportunity to refresh your business when required and take advantage of new and emerging markets. If you truly want to expand, you need to avoid parking your business at its trading ceiling. The big message here is that you need to be able to see clearly where you can go. Business leaders and their marketers need to be constantly ahead of the current business model, both testing and challenging their current thinking in order to grow. It requires the leader to remain focused on the "what". The longer you take to open your eyes to the risk of stagnation, the greater the potential cost to your business. In fact, in the airline industry example, many established market leaders lost their position for good. Rebuilding your brand from scratch is a considerably different proposition to refreshing an already successful business. Investing in well-structured strategic plans removes any reliance on organic growth and sidesteps these potential roadblocks to sustained success.

And how does strategic planning relate to the leadership models we've explored? Well-produced, consistently-structured, high-level strategic plans are the backbone of any organisation that is looking to operate within the leader-leader model. They are the ultimate tool in gaining that all important high alignment and high autonomy. They allow senior leaders to set clear parameters and boundaries, which offers the team the clarity they require to operate freely and demonstrate their skill and competency.

Before we look further at the structure of an effective strategic plan, it is important to remind ourselves why so many plans fail to deliver. As I've said before, understanding the breadth and depth of your team is critical in the creation of high-quality plans and is part of the alignment process. You will need a high level of autonomy across your teams if you want to run multiple

Chapter 8: The Value of Strategic Planning

strategic plans in your business. And, as discussed in the chapter regarding failure, the plan must be in the right hands in terms of experience and skill, supported by a high level of discipline to see it through. If you want your plan to succeed, avoid engaging the slightly incompetent person who lacks self-discipline. When plans are at a strategic level, they require the approach of the skipper's navigational expert: an experienced person who is a master of direction, and whose clear intent is to arrive at the desired destination. Plan management is a key trait in a strong leader, and a dedicated planning framework offers considerable opportunity to guide and develop others.

I truly believe that this is where business can draw a lot of lessons from the world of professional sport, as well as the armed and emergency services. In these fields, there is an innate approach to discipline which is necessary when it comes to strategic planning and embedding that plan effectively. This doesn't mean that you need to adopt the sergeant major approach to management, but you should be mindful of the fact that the business world struggles to stay on track in terms of plan management. During the 2012 London Olympics, the British rowing team reached its peak and topped the medal table with nine, including four golds. Far from sitting on their laurels, the coaching team immediately set about underpinning this success and put together a strategic plan to seek out new talent through the Start Programme initiative. They knew that selection was key. More than 30,000 people signed up on "learn to row" courses, an unprecedented take-up. From that, 1,000 individuals were selected for the Start Programme, with 350 put through their paces by British rowing chiefs. Four years later, they again topped the medal table at the Rio Olympics. Sport at this high level understands the value of refreshing its approach in order to maintain its competitive edge. They looked outside their normal procedure and developed a successful strategy to attract new talent.

As with these disciplined fields, you need to create an environment where enacting the plan becomes the natural approach within your business. It requires input and energy to maintain, so it needs to be part of the everyday momentum of each team. It must also be ardently desired at the highest level if it is to succeed. The overreliance on traditional key performance indicators (KPIs) seems to prevent some businesses from creating new plans that challenge them. It is those KPIs that often drive you to the trading ceilings discussed earlier. It takes courage to challenge the numbers (KPIs) that have driven you to previous success. We have a habit of accepting their validity because of familiarity, comfort and internal industry logic. However, many KPIs are formed and underpinned by either a business' own trading history or recognised industry statistics. If you use them in isolation to form future opinions, you can easily miss changing environments and unwittingly apply an outdated measurement that restricts growth. When the mobile phone industry boomed, KPIs forecasted that the market was reaching a saturation level in terms of mobile phone ownership. Those technology companies that looked beyond this indicator, however, realised that the new emerging market was about making the mobile phone more than just a phone. Some companies were left behind, with only their historic KPIs to reflect on. It is this level of strategic planning that creates real growth which your shareholders can value in terms of investment. The process alone forces you to challenge the status quo and, if crafted and executed well, it engages the whole business on a more enlightened journey.

At sea, the skipper needs to arrive at the chosen destination, and the plan needs to be executed. If we could find this clarity in business and focus our energies only on the strategy that will deliver our priorities, where the goal is paramount and the stakes high, we may be able to achieve great things. If a leader can inspire and motivate with a plan like this, they will create alignment with the team so they truly understand and share in the value of success and the potential cost of failure.

Putting it into practice:

- Can you see the limits of your current business model?
- When was the last time you challenged the validity of your KPIs?
- Can you see outside your bias based on internal industry logic?
- Does your strategy plan consider diversification and innovation?

Chapter 9

An Example of a Typical Planning Framework

Now that we understand the value of strategic planning and the role of the skipper or business leader in this process, we can consider what a planning framework might look like. We will explore a typical set of key components that need to be in place in order to move our proposal to an actual plan of activity.

I must warn you – do not write any proposal that lacks gravitas. Quite simply, the potential outcome of the plan needs to be truly valued and desired by the sponsor in order for it to be adopted and embedded. As skippers, we do not waste our time developing plans to destinations that we are not really planning to visit. I apologise if that sounds like an obvious statement, but you would be surprised by the amount of business plans that are sanctioned without true intent. Also, ensure it is written in simple, clear and precise language, avoiding gobbledygook, jargon, unnecessarily long words and padding. I was once subjected to a business owner who, having followed a course on how to write a successful plan, became obsessed with how it was to be written. So much attention was given to the words used, the tense in which it was written and the grammar, that by the time the plans were complete, which were all woefully late, all momentum and interest had been lost in the process of production. Each and every one had an eventual slow death. Factual and measurable content is all that is required.

Let's consider the key components, one by one.

1. Proposal validation

The proposal needs to be drafted at a level of clarity that allows the key stakeholders to validate its purpose before the plan is built. The temptation is to overbuild a plan before the purpose has been truly validated as worthwhile by the business, but this can lead to wasted effort. Once researched, simply set out an overview of the proposed plan with a clear final destination, add three to five quality gateway objectives and an overview of the supporting numbers. The basic proposal should be no more than two sheets of A4, preferably just one.

The process of preparing a proposal should force the concept to be challenged by both the sponsor and those senior team members that will ultimately be responsible for its execution. This is not about the words we choose; this is about clearly laying out a realistic and potentially achievable goal. Investing quality time at this research stage is key and, as a leader, you need to create an environment that allows clear thought during this early part of the process. Consider the fact that you are likely to be planning to proceed in a direction that may be unfamiliar to the business. Thus, you have to be able to clearly demonstrate that you can navigate your way there in order to reach the goals outlined.

In terms of alignment, the proposal and validation steps are key to underpinning the plan from the very outset of its life. There may be a need to sell the plan to the wider business at a later stage, but for now, it needs to have the support of your direct team.

Chapter 9: An Example of a Typical Planning Framework

It is this level of discipline that is required from the outset. Remember, the professional skipper is an expert at arriving. They design and shape a passage plan that is based on reality in the knowledge that, if the situation dictates that a deviation is required in order to maintain the overall goal, they will simply accommodate a route alteration that offers greater clarity and set about reshaping the course to the original destination. Other than the completely unknown, most potential alterations off course are covered and considered in the initial passage plan. Therefore, the navigator's role is often to apply the strategic alternative. They are naturally geared to expect the unexpected.

2. **The "who"**

   Initially, every plan needs three key individuals that are required to act as the foundation and owners of the complete planning process:

   - The skipper (sponsor in business terms) – this individual normally holds the purse strings and is responsible for sanctioning the resources required to complete the plan. They are accountable for the ultimate return on investment and, often, they are the visionary for the plan itself.

   - The navigator (plan or project manager in business terms) – they are responsible for the overall shaping of the plan and driving it through to completion. They work with the skipper to select and recruit the senior team.

   - The plan administrator – they work with all parties and are responsible for recording and monitoring the performance. They continually update the live information as it becomes available, producing reports on progress towards key gateways and offer support to the skipper and navigator in terms of administrative tasks.

Let's dig a little deeper into the details of the "who" and the dos and don'ts that might help or hinder your success. The skipper is typically the business owner, director, department head or a senior leader. Depending on the size of your organisation or team, the skipper and navigator could in fact be the same person. In our Fastnet team, the type of challenge and number of crew warranted a standalone navigator to support the skipper.

If the plan is of a size that requires multiple skippers (as in a fleet of yachts with a common goal), this is a clear indication that you might need to consider breaking down the plan into smaller components. If this issue is left unchallenged, there is a real risk of too many communication lines at a high level, all of which will lead to a lack of alignment and autonomy. There will be too many "whos" for it to work in practice. If your strategic plan is about a large shift in direction, or one that affects many people within your organisation, it is far better to have an overarching plan which is then supported by, and which feeds into, a number of complementary smaller strategic plans. In this way, each part of the activity relies on just one leader and their direct team working as a more manageable unit but towards the overall business goal. However, it is important that all these plans have the same basic structure as the overarching framework so that they are consistent and align in purpose and approach. The teams who enact these smaller strategic plans need to understand the role of the skipper and, in order to be fully aligned, they must be clear on the principles behind the plan, its parameters and who is accountable for which outcomes. Agreeing those all-important boundaries and parameters are key in allowing high levels of autonomy in terms of task achieving, budgets, timelines etc.

Most importantly, and this statement needs to continually echo in your ears, do not compromise on the skill of the skipper. That's if you really want to have the best chance of success for a plan that offers strategic value to the business. Those that are highly risk averse, procrastinate over decision-making or are unable to be fully accountable for potential failure need not apply. Managing strategic planning has inherent risks, and an individual that navigates in a style of excessive cautiousness, that "dumbs down" the destination or, worse, holds the team accountable for navigating errors, is not going to grow your business or sail you into unfamiliar waters that offer such rich potential. You need someone of exceptional vision who can merge both discipline and creativity to achieve greatness.

I've mentioned the phrase 'journey seeker' a number of times in this book, and it's worth revisiting here. In the context of strategic planning, they are perhaps the worst choice of skipper you could make. On an endless journey of discovery, they have no end goal and thus no passage plan. In this way, they avoid accountability and the taint of failure as the destination is unknown: quite an appealing prospect for the risk-averse. They also often attract like-minded teams who struggle to make decisions or tangible progress. When the environment you are working within requires you to attain various gateways and milestones in order to proceed, you need leaders who are attuned to making directional decisions and who inspire their teams to use their initiative towards executing a plan autonomously. In simple terms, you need leadership who can successfully navigate from A to B.

Once the proposal has been validated by the skipper, in collaboration with the navigator, they need to recruit a small specialist team of highly-skilled individuals – senior leaders. They will work up the detail of the strategic plan, focusing on the key objectives, and be responsible for the plan's activation throughout the business. This small team should be completely accountable for the perceived value of the plan by the wider business, ensuring that the ultimate goal is embedded throughout and that its relationship to the objectives is clearly understood by each team. The high alignment and high autonomy model should allow each leader throughout the business with responsibility for embedding the plan to interpret the details in order to successfully motivate their teams, all in pursuit of a common purpose.

3. **Structuring the plan: setting tasks, objectives and the final destination**

Now assume that your initial proposal has been validated and you are good to go. It is now a case of laying out the basic detail. This consists of identifying the general route and each key gateway or milestone (objectives) and then adding the basic activities (tasks) required to gain momentum. Once the task list has been adopted by the appropriate personnel and the necessary detail has been added by them, the skipper appraises the overall plan, makes provision for potential alterations and sets it in motion. As leader, it is crucial that

Chapter 9: An Example of a Typical Planning Framework

every key objective in the plan is measurable and each task can be delegated so that it works in a practical context.

The three main components to the structure are as follows:

- The **destination** – A clear description of the overall goal and anticipated timeframe for reaching it.
- Three to five **objectives** that represent the key gateways and milestones that move you towards the destination.
- Five to Ten **tasks** or activities that contribute to the successful completion of each objective.

The diagram in Figure 9.1 on page 105 is a typical example of the basic structure of a plan. It is in fact a visual breakdown of our preparation strategy for our Fastnet campaign. You can clearly see it has one main goal, our destination, which is to get to the start line of this iconic race. That is then supported by three key objectives, all of which act as clear gateways towards our overall ambition. Each one of the objectives is owned by a senior player within the team.

In this example, the objectives are supported by a list of 10 tasks. These represent an overview of the general activity required in order to progress. It is really important not to overdo the detail at this stage, as you will look to the wider team to add this. What's more important is the value of the statement in terms of guaranteeing momentum. By this I mean the objectives must be clear in their intent of guaranteeing progress. Hence why this is often referred to as a milestone (a significant stage in the overall journey). You need to ensure your objectives have been clearly defined. Each task is then delegated to the wider team, all of whom understand and are aligned with the overall purpose of the plan. It is at this point that the detail can be added to each task by the person responsible for its outcome.

In terms of communicating the plan, the skipper would have briefed their direct team who are accountable for achieving each one of the objectives. They would then have back briefed the skipper with their understanding of the plan in order to ensure full alignment. The skipper's direct team would then set about briefing their teams in exactly the same fashion, this time using the task list as an overview of the activity and the objectives as their clear gateway to the main destination.

You know what is coming next. It is imperative that each level of leadership in this process has the skill set and autonomy to carry out their tasks independently and within the parameters and boundaries agreed. In terms of strategic business plans, these boundaries are mainly agreed timelines and financial considerations.

It's also essential that those responsible for achieving the tasks fully embrace and understand the ultimate destination and how each milestone provides a foundation on which to get one step closer to that end goal. That way, they have clear sight of the purpose that is driving them, allowing them to address the tasks as they see fit in order to maintain momentum.

This overall approach and framework, if managed and communicated correctly, offers the ideal environment for high levels of alignment and autonomy.

Chapter 9: An Example of a Typical Planning Framework

Destination
Enter the RORC Fastnet yacht race and arrive at the start line with an amateur offshore racing team

	Objective 1 - Equipment Procure a suitable offshore yacht suitable for a crew of 8		**Objective 2 - People** Recruit and train the crew members		**Objective 3 - Admin** Set up a shore-based administration team
No.	**Task**	**No.**	**Task**	**No.**	**Task**
1	Research a number of suitable yacht designs. Make and model.	1	Advertise programme to interested parties. Expressing limited numbers.	1	Recruit an admin leader for the complete campaign.
2	Visit yacht charter companies and view suitable examples.	2	Research RORC training and experience requirements.	2	Set up and agree an overall budget to cover all expenses.
3	Talk to and visit local boat owners who may have a suitable yacht.	3	Confirm selection of candidates. Based on team composition requirements.	3	Make an application to RORC and secure a place.
4	List out and procure safety equipment. Including RORC supplied tracker.	4	Organise specialist compliance training. Sea survival, first aid etc.	4	Set up a project progress tracker. Feedback loop for task completion.
5	Research and procure communications and navigation equipment.	5	Set up and agree dates for team training weekends and navigation strategy days.	5	Seek out sponsor for branded team clothing.
6	Design and distribute the minimum kit list to all crew. Including branded clothing.	6	Design a complete onboard practical training programme.	6	Set up a campaign funding payment plan for all crew members.
7	Design victuals requirements for training weekends and the race itself.	7	Select candidates for key roles. Skipper, navigator and watch leaders x 2.	7	Collate all personal details and contact info from crew. Including health and dietary.
8	Procure victuals in line with activity programme.	8	Recruit outside assistance for specialist onboard training modules.	8	Agree protocol for shore-based communication during training and the race.
9	Consider/plan for minimum supporting equipment in terms of race weight.	9	Design and implement watch system for training weekends and the race.	9	Set up feedback loop for family and friends during the race.
10	Design and implement equipment checklist prior to all offshore activities.	10	Set out a clear preparation programme for final day before race start.	10	Organise welcoming party on completion of race.

Figure 9.1 Our strategic plan for our Fastnet race preparation

4. **Plan administration**

   You may recall my comments in the earlier section regarding passage planning and how it is an imperfect predictor of what will happen in reality. The skipper is aware that the moment the yacht slips its moorings and heads out onto the open sea, the plan becomes fluid and is subject to many unknowns. This is when plan administration comes into play; the art of enacting the strategy day to day in the sometimes-stormy seas.

   In my experience, the reality for most well-considered business plans is that maintaining momentum becomes the biggest challenge. Understanding and accepting that you may have to alter course from time to time is essential. As with a ship's log, it is critical to regularly measure and record your progress in achieving tasks to maintain momentum. In this way, you can quickly recognise when you aren't going to meet objectives by critiquing live information and, importantly, you can hold task leaders accountable. If you adopt this approach, you'll ensure that you are always one step ahead of the plan. Ignoring how we are progressing at any point is a potentially suicidal step in the world of the skipper. That is why it rarely happens. When the stakes are high (as it should be when it comes to a strategic plan), do not lose sight of the destination and maintain a disciplined approach to plan management.

   In the past, I have adopted a simple but effective measurement tool that allows me and other leaders a snapshot view of progress. Within a basic excel spreadsheet, I capture the timeline and budget expectations for each task and I weight each component with a percentage value in terms of its contribution to the overall goal.

Chapter 9: An Example of a Typical Planning Framework

In the example of the Fastnet plan, each objective had a value of 30%, and therefore each one of the 10 tasks per objective was valued at 3%. In terms of this particular example, we had around 10 months to fulfil all our objectives. Every three months we needed to have achieved at least 30% value across all tasks in order to be on track. Eventually, and right up to until the day before the race, we needed to have achieved all of our objectives and be 90% complete when it came to our tasks. We valued getting to the start line on time at 10%, bringing us to 100% complete and ready to go when the start gun was sounded.

As an aside, it is important, as a leader, if you need to abort the plan, assuming there are no alternative routes to your chosen destination, that you do so at the earliest opportunity. This ensures you limit the resources used on a wasted journey. All good leaders know how to take such decisions, whilst maintaining the respect and trust of their team.

Putting it into practice:

- How could this simple planning framework work for you and your team?
- Think about what components have been missing in your previous strategic plans and how they might have held you back.
- Why do you think plans lose their momentum, and what can we do to maintain direction?
- Are you able to isolate yourself from time to time in order to clearly review progress towards your goal?

Final Thoughts

In this book, I set out to share my take on the correlation between the effective skipper at sea and the professional leader in the world of business. Ultimately, it is all about the combination of effective leadership of people and a robust strategic plan, the combination of which will get you to those all-important milestones and, ultimately, your final goal. If you want your plans to succeed, then set the stakes high and make sure the destination is truly desired by the drivers of the plan. Reward them well when you arrive and have the discipline to hold others accountable for their contribution during the journey. Standing still or relying on organic growth is a not an option in today's fast-paced world of business. We are faced with an abundance of opportunity, but still we need to underpin our approach with the basics of getting the team right and executing well-thought-out plans. There is certainly something to be said for becoming a master of arriving.

I want to leave you with a final reflection that may draw together the spirit of all we've covered so far in the book. When I skipper a sailing yacht during a typical day at sea, I will get up in the morning and walk around so I can see the team at work and survey the environment that we are in. I will look through the log and read the report on recent activity. I will meet the navigator and appraise the plan, and together we will forecast what we expect in the days ahead, updating the strategy as required. Later I will brief the watch leaders on what we are looking to achieve and ask them to work up their plan of action, add the detail, brief

SHIPSHAPE

their teams and return to me with a back brief. During the day I will look at areas of constraint or improvement and work with my direct team to aid and guide their learning. At the end of my watch period, I will hand over to the on-watch leader and sleep well in the knowledge that we are fully aligned and the team has the autonomy to add the detail and carry out the actions required to maintain our direction.

As leader of my day-to-day business team, I will do exactly the same as above – but this time on dry land.

Good luck with crafting your business passage plan. Recruit and employ the best talent to execute it with you, and have the discipline to see it through. If you would like to know more about implementing the frameworks we have discussed in the book, or would like to experience the value of what the sea has to offer in terms of accelerated learning for you and your teams, I would be only too pleased to help.